THE GRACE OF COMING HOME

THE
GRACE OF COMING HOME

Spirituality, Sexuality, and the Struggle for Justice

Melanie Morrison

The Pilgrim Press
Cleveland, Ohio

The Pilgrim Press, Cleveland, Ohio 44115
© 1995 by Melanie Morrison

Printed in the United States of America on acid-free paper

00 99 98   5 4 3 2

Library of Congress Cataloging-in-Publication Data
Morrison, Melanie, 1949–
      The grace of coming home : spirituality, sexuality, and the
  struggle for justice / Melanie Morrison.
          p.   cm.
      Includes bibliographical references and index.
      ISBN 0-8298-1071-4 (alk. paper)
      1. Feminist theology.   2. Lesbianism—Religious aspects—
  Christianity.   3. Christianity and justice.   4. Morrison, Melanie,
  1949–   .   5. Lesbians—Religious life.   I. Title.
  BT83.55.M67   1995
  230'.082—dc20   95-18070
                                                              CIP

To April,
beloved life companion

In Memoriam

*To Audre Lorde,
who knew that our silence
will not protect us*

We are all the Creator's children.

We didn't come out of the past unhurt,

but together, individually and through our cultures,

we can heal our world and bring each other home . . .

And remember, we want to make sure

that we all come home together.

—MARIE-THÉRÈSE "TESS" BROWNE

CONTENTS

Acknowledgments   xi
Introduction   xiii

I. Coming Home   1
   1. Standing on Holy Ground   3
   2. A Crisis of Pronouns   7
   3. Singing Hope's Song in a Strange Land   14
   4. The Heart of the Matter   20
   5. You Are My Beloved   27
   6. Creating New Rituals:
      Rites of Passage in Lesbian and Gay
      Communities   33

II. Grace Reveals a New Name   43
   7. The Power of Saying God–She   45
   8. Good Shame/Bad Shame   49
   9. Humility Reconsidered   58
   10. The Cross and the Triangle   62
   11. In This *Kairos* Moment   66
   12. Sophia's Friends   75

III. Resurrection Stories   77
      13. Rising like the Phoenix:
           A New Church Movement   79
      14. A Human Being Fully Alive   86
      15. Remembering Re-Imagining   92
      16. What We Can (and Cannot) Do for
           One Another   97
      17. A Time to Mourn and a Time to Dance   103
      18. Letter to Audre   108

IV. A Love That Won't Let Go   113
      19. In the Presence of My Enemies: A Communion
           Meditation   115
      20. Godwrestling   121
      21. Is It Okay to Be Happy?   127
      22. Refraining from Explaining   133
      23. Telling the Truth about Our Lives   139
      24. The Pearl of Great Price   142

Notes   149
Credits   155
Bibliography   159
Index   163

ACKNOWLEDGMENTS

I have had the privilege of working these past several years with different communities of people where questions of spirituality, sexuality, and justice have been honored and intensively scrutinized. This means I have been gifted with many spiritual companions and theological partners who have informed and inspired the writing of this book.

I am grateful to the women and men of Phoenix Community Church in Kalamazoo, Michigan, who had the audacity and courage to set out on a journey together with few maps or models. Serving as one of the pastors of this new church was an experience that stretched and strengthened me in unimaginable ways. The questions, struggles, hopes, and wisdom of the Phoenix people are reflected throughout this book.

I could not begin to name the many people I have been privileged to meet and learn from at Leaven retreats, seminars, and workshops. Especially, I want to acknowledge the clergywomen who, over the past six years, have gathered monthly in the seminar called Sister Colleagues. In the holy space we create together, no theological question has been considered too heretical or too orthodox. In the telling and hearing of our stories, we have borne each other's rage at the ways the church still harms women. We also have celebrated together whenever a sister experienced breakthrough, transformation, and healing.

My spirit has been nurtured by the wild and wonderful women of CLOUT (Christian Lesbians OUT Together). During that first gathering in New York in 1990 when ten of us dreamed CLOUT into being, I experienced a profound homecoming. I found sisters who called me by name and with whom I could speak in my native tongue. Every CLOUT gathering since has been a delight. I am so thankful for the prophetic courage, outrageous humor, and theological daring of these sisters.

Another community that has supported and challenged me is the United Church Coalition for Lesbian and Gay Concerns. I am especially grateful to Jan Griesinger, indefatigable prophet within the United Church of Christ.

There are a number of women whose writings have been life changing for me as they helped me find, and speak in, my lesbian feminist voice: Barbara Deming, Marilyn Frye, Carter Heyward, Audre Lorde, and Adrienne Rich.

I wish to thank a number of dear friends who have been theological partners and mentors through the years: CathyAnn Beaty, Riet Bons-Storm, Cyril Colonius, Katie Day, Anneke Geense-Ravestein, Tine Kamphuis, Aukje Krol, Rob van Kessel, Phyl Landick, Janna van Loon, Barbara Lundblad, Laura Mol, and Lynnette Stallworth.

Three people deserve special thanks for their immeasurable support and encouragement: my partner April Allison, whose gifts as a writer and editor informed this project; and Eleanor and Truman Morrison, colleagues and parents, who model for me an obstinate hope and untiring commitment in the struggle for justice.

It has been a delight to work with the people at The Pilgrim Press. I am thankful for Richard Brown's passion, vision, and skill as editor. Both he and Marjorie Pon have been accessible, candid, and exceptionally helpful throughout the process.

INTRODUCTION

In 1990, I was asked to be one of the speakers at the Michigan Lesbian and Gay Pride March. Even though I suspected I had been asked because I am an openly lesbian ordained minister, I wrote the first drafts of my speech without any mention of the word "Christian." I was hesitant to come out as a Christian in front of thousands of lesbian and gay people, most of whom did not know me personally.

I feared being stereotyped and written off. I had ample experience of how the word "Christian" functioned as a barrier rather than a bridge. Identifying as Christian appeared to make me an ally of people with whom I have nothing in common except the name. Especially in the presence of lesbians and gay men, but also with my feminist sisters, I was shy about coming out as a Christian because it is Christians who have declared us "the enemy."

Feelings of grief, shame, and rage also made me reluctant to come out as a Christian. I carry an abiding grief because my female and lesbian ancestors have been victims of violence at the hands of the church. I carry shame as a white North American Christian for the way my tradition has been used to sanction racism and colonial oppression. I share the rage that many of my lesbian sisters and gay brothers feel toward the church. It is in churches that we often hear that who we are and who we love are considered an abomination in God's sight.

For too many years, I tried to speak about myself in the church without saying, "I am a lesbian," until I realized I could not speak in my own voice or live with integrity unless I was both visible and verbal *as* a lesbian. In similar fashion, but for different reasons, I was trying to speak about myself in lesbian and gay communities without saying, "I am a Christian."

Shortly before the Pride March, while I was still struggling to write my speech, I attended a lecture by Audre Lorde. She introduced herself by saying, "I am a black, lesbian, feminist, poet, mother, warrior doing her work. . . . Who are you?"

Her question, "Who are you?" jolted me into remembering that my work (meaning my deepest spiritual and human vocation) is shaped by my social location: my skin color, gender, class, and sexual orientation. My work is also shaped by my chosen loyalties, commitments, and values, including my feminism and my Christian faith. My "work" as a Christian is profoundly influenced by the fact that I am a lesbian feminist, and my work as a lesbian feminist is profoundly influenced by the fact that I am a Christian.

Who I am informs what my work is and where I will do it. I am not African American—I am white; and that fact means that my work can never be the same as Audre Lorde's work. We can both be about the work of antiracism, but how we do that work and where we do it will probably vary by virtue of our skin color. Part of my work as a white, feminist, lesbian, North American Christian is to keep making the connections between racism, sexism, classism, and heterosexism—even when, and especially when, those connections force me to acknowledge my own complicity in the structures of oppression and call me to change. As Audre Lorde also asked that night: "Are you willing to use the power that you have in the service of what you say you believe in?"

On those Capitol steps, I answered Audre Lorde's questions by beginning my speech: "I am a white, lesbian, feminist, Christian minister doing her work." I chose to come out as a Christian because I do not want to distance myself from my grief, shame, and rage. I chose to come out as a Christian because it is not *only* grief, shame, and rage that I feel.

If I found Christianity oppressive and deadening at its core, I would not stay—even though it is my heritage. I choose to stay because many of the images, stories, and themes are liberating and life giving for me: images such as exodus and resurrection, faith as a journey, the yearning for justice and a promised land, the notion that God is in our choices *for* life and *against* death, the notion that love and justice are inseparable, the belief that there is a source of life and love at the heart of the universe that yearns for our healing and wholeness and liberation and that is grieved when we are less than we can be.

As a lesbian, feminist Christian, I find myself by relegation and by choice on the margins of the institutional church. From that place, part of my work is to name the parts of the Christian tradition that have been destructive to lesbians and gay men and to call the church to account for its sins against us. Another part of my work is to encourage my lesbian sisters and gay brothers to proudly, boldly claim the spiritual wisdom and gifts that are ours. Yet another part is to articulate what there is in Christianity that is liberating and life giving for me as a lesbian.

I do not feel at home in many Christian churches. But I do feel at home with against-the-stream, liberation-oriented Christians around the world. I think of friends who risk going to jail because they will not pay taxes to the Pentagon; I think of Murphy Davis and Ed Weir, who have been visiting prisoners on death row in Georgia for years; I think of Christians in South Africa who risked imprisonment, torture, and death in their resistance to apartheid; I think of womanist and feminist liberation theologians like Delores Williams, Katie Cannon, Rosemary Ruether, and Carter Heyward; I think of the wild, outrageous women of CLOUT (Christian Lesbians OUT Together) who proudly, brazenly celebrate the miracle of being lesbian, Christian, and out.

I also feel at home with the many sisters and brothers I have been privileged to meet through my work, over the past seven years, with an organization called Leaven and with Phoenix Community Church.

In 1986, I returned to the United States after living in the Netherlands for five years. After a period of intense self-scrutiny, I realized I could no longer tolerate the closet and decided to pursue only those work arenas where I could be out as a lesbian. My employment options were suddenly significantly reduced. At that time, I began to explore creating a nonprofit organization with my colleague and mother, Eleanor S. Morrison. She is a skilled designer and facilitator of groups, and I wanted to work as an apprentice, learning those skills firsthand. She had years of experience teaching and writing about human sexuality in university and church settings. She is also an ordained minister in the United Church of Christ.

In 1987, we launched Leaven, a nonprofit organization that provides education, resources, and training in the areas of feminism, spiritual development, and sexual justice. Leaven is committed to helping create a context for grass-roots feminist reflection, study, and dialogue, exploring the vitality and wisdom of spirituality that is rooted in a passion for justice. Individually and as a team, Eleanor Morrison and I lead seminars, workshops, training events, and retreats.

As we travel around the country, we encounter women and men who are hungry for a mature spirituality and theology. A number of the topics addressed in this book are inspired by the questions that we hear people ask again and again.

- Why is male language for God considered orthodox and female language for God so often considered heretical?
- If you take patriarchy out of Christianity, is the heart still beating?
- If I cannot affirm the statement, "No one comes to the Father except through me," am I still a Christian?
- How can I honestly acknowledge and understand the centuries of violence perpetrated by Christian churches against women, Jews, gay men, and lesbians?
- If I cannot embrace traditional Christian teachings about original sin and atonement theology, is there a place for me within the Christian church?

- Are there resources in the Christian faith that can bring us into right relationship with the earth?

When seekers find a safe context in which to ask such questions aloud and to search with others for answers, they experience a profound sense of relief, realizing that they are not alone. We often hear people say: "I thought I was the only one who had this question, and I was afraid to voice it. But now I hear there are others who are seeking, who yearn to reimagine their faith."

Shortly after we began Leaven, my friend and colleague Cyril Colonius was forced to leave the congregation he had served for six years—solely because he is gay. In the aftermath of that dismissal, Cyril and I talked about starting a new church community that would welcome all people, including lesbians and gay men. In February 1988, on Ash Wednesday evening, eighteen people gathered in Cyril's living room in Kalamazoo, Michigan, to begin conversation about forming a new congregation. We chose the name Phoenix Community Church as a symbol of the hope that gave birth to this church. I was asked to serve part-time, along with Cyril, as one of the pastors, and I remained there for the next five years.

This book, composed during the last seven years of work with Leaven and Phoenix Community Church, is a collection of essays, addresses, meditations, and sermons, pulled together with two primary groups of readers in mind. I am writing for lesbians and gay men who feel they are faced with an impossible choice: to surrender part of their deepest identity, either as self-affirming and proud lesbian/gay people or as Christians. I want you to hear and know that you are not alone; that there are others of us who have faced this wrenching choice and who have refused to make it.

I also am writing for women and men—of whatever sexual orientation—who have felt alienated from the church and Christian tradition by virtue of noninclusive language, fear-based images of God, and disempowering images of humanity. There are so many of us searching for a spirituality that honors our deepest questions and sustains us in the struggle for justice. Many of the pieces in this book are story-based; and some are autobiographical, in the hope that my experience will intersect and resonate with your own. I share with you my attempts to reimagine and rearticulate, from a feminist perspective, theological concepts such as sin, grace, and resurrection, and I offer what I have learned from encountering scripture as a lesbian feminist.

The title of this book, *The Grace of Coming Home*, needs to be placed in its intended context lest it be heard as the nostalgic yearning to return to one's birthplace or to an idealized fantasy of some time past. The homecoming of which I speak is glimpsed in the present, but it has a decidedly "not yet" character. One glimpses this homecoming every time one confronts and challenges racism or names abuse of power, every time a person comes out, and every time a woman finds her voice. Even though, as Tess Browne says, "we didn't come out of the past unhurt," it is possible to find the courage and the grace to "heal our world and bring each other home." Yet not until every person is accorded justice and freedom from oppression in all its forms can we speak of a true homecoming. For as Tess Browne so eloquently reminds us, we must all come home together.

I was inspired to write this book by the courage and faith of sisters and brothers who dare to claim the dissonances and complexities of their lives and to proudly wear their many—sometimes seemingly contradictory—names. Brave women and men from many different spiritual traditions have whispered to me: "Don't let them steal what's yours. Don't let anyone impose his or her choices on you. Don't let anyone do your own naming." I am surrounded by a great cloud of coconspirators who breathe with me and encourage me to subvert every oppressive choice.[1]

With many coconspiring sisters and brothers, I choose to stay on the margins of the Christian tradition, neither distancing myself completely from it nor severing my critical relationship to it. With some fear and trembling, I can still say: "I am a white, lesbian, feminist, Christian minister doing her work."

Who are you?

I

COMING HOME

1

STANDING ON
HOLY GROUND

You probably have a place, some special place, that may look very ordinary to others but to you is very precious because of something that happened there—an encounter in which you realized beyond all doubt that you were not alone and that you were loved. That special place may be a room in a house, a restaurant, a beach, or a forest where you once walked with a friend. While you were walking, you found the courage to say out loud things you had never dared to say to another person for fear of being misunderstood or judged. But as you struggled to find the words and you spoke them from the heart, your friend touched your arm lightly and nodded as though to say, "It's okay, you needn't be afraid. What you're telling me doesn't shock me or change the way I feel about you."

At that moment, in that place, you had a sense of coming home, of being found. It was as though you heard your name spoken as never before.

Or maybe you were all alone in a forest, on a beach, or in a room, yet you sensed a presence, you felt called by name, and you knew that you were loved for yourself. And you have never quite been the same since. Not because there are no more times of grief or doubt or disappointment, but because that memory of grace remains. Whether you physically return to that place or not, you return there in memory, because ever since that moment, that place is uniquely special. You could say it has become holy ground.

For someone who wasn't there at that moment, your place may seem quite ordinary—just another room, restaurant, beach, or

forest. It is hard to explain why this particular place is special, holy—
as difficult as it must have been for Moses to explain his encounter
by a desert bush.

Imagine if Moses had taken his father-in-law, Jethro, back to
that spot in the desert. Chances are, Jethro would have looked at
Moses and said, "Yeah, so is this the place you were talking about?
What's so special about this place? I just see an old bush like all the
other bushes around here. Why have you brought me here?"

Moses might have had a hard time convincing Jethro that he
was standing on holy ground. Moses had no proof of what had
happened there. He had no ashes to show that the bush had been
burning. Moses could only stand there with empty hands and tell his
story: that he had felt called by name as never before and that he had
heard God's name revealed. He could only point to that bush and
say: "Here is where it all began. It was here that I knew I'd have to
go to Pharaoh and demand that he let our people go. I was terrified
at the thought; I didn't know what I would say to Pharaoh. But I
also knew that I wouldn't be alone, because it was here that I learned
the name of God—I AM WHO I AM—I Will Be There For You."

To Moses that day was revealed God's heart and that which
grieves God: "I have seen the affliction of my people who are in
Egypt. I have heard their cries. I know their sufferings and I have
come to deliver them out of the hand of the Egyptians." Moses
understood that day that to love God is to know what grieves God,
just as to love another person is to know that person's pain.

There is a Hasidic story about a conversation between two
villagers:

> The first said: "Tell me, friend Ivan, do you love me?"
> The second: "I love you deeply."
> The first: "Do you know, my friend, what gives me pain?"
> The second: "How can I, pray, know what gives you pain?"
> The first: "If you do not know what gives me pain, how can
> you say that you truly love me?"[1]

The gift Moses received that day, in the intimate encounter by
the bush, was to hear of God's pain. Moses not only heard God's

pain, but heard that something had to be done and that he, Moses, was to do it.

Reflecting on this encounter at the burning bush, I'm reminded of an experience in seminary, in which I was in the midst of a crisis, overwhelmed by anxiety, swallowed up in pain. Too many people responded to me at the time by saying, "Oh, don't take it so seriously, Melanie. Before you know it, you'll be your old, cheerful self again." Statements like that weren't comforting; they left me feeling more isolated and alone.

I had a professor who impressed me as someone wise and possessing a deep personal faith. I'd never spoken to her outside of class, but one day I decided that I needed to talk with her. Because I couldn't imagine what I would say or how I'd get started, I walked around campus for an hour or so, fighting my shyness and doubt.

When I finally stood in the open door of her office, she didn't see me. I breathed deeply and whispered "hello." She looked up and greeted me as if she had been waiting for me: "Melanie!" (I didn't even know she had connected my face with a name.) "Come in," she said. "Come in and sit down."

I sat down, but couldn't think of a thing to say. I could only sigh and look around the room with panic. She took her chair from behind her desk and set it next to mine, facing in the same direction I faced. There we sat, beside one another, for some moments in silence. Then she asked, very softly, very gently, how I was.

"Not so good," I said. "I feel very scared. I can't explain this terrible anxiety that has hold of me, but I had the feeling I should come here and talk with you. . . . I can't explain why. . . ."

"You don't need to explain," she said, "I'm just happy you came."

Several more moments passed in silence. She made me a cup of tea. Every so often, I found a few words to express myself. She listened and never tried, even once, to offer any solutions or push my feelings away. She didn't get up and go to her bookshelf to locate a title on anxiety and faith.

After some time, I said that perhaps I should be going. She said, "You may come back any time you wish. You don't even need to say anything. We can just sit here next to one another, so that you will know anyway that you are not alone."

If you were to ask me what this person did for me, I would say: she was there for me. In a time when I felt immeasurably heavy— too heavy for another person to bear—she carried me, conveying, without words, three things: "I hear your pain; I take it seriously; but this pain is not your destiny."

Only for an hour or so did I sit there in that ordinary room, drinking an ordinary cup of tea. As far as I can remember, the name of God was never spoken aloud. But that room will always be holy ground for me—holy ground on which I did, in fact, hear the name of God: I AM WHO I AM. I Will Be There For You.

2

A   CRISIS   OF   PRONOUNS

When I returned to the United States after living in the Netherlands for five years, it was like starting over again. I considered "candidating" at various churches seeking a minister, and I explored teaching in a seminary. But I knew that my chances of obtaining either position would be greatly increased by hiding one important fact about myself—that I am a lesbian.

I hadn't revealed my sexual orientation to anyone except my family and a small circle of friends. This was a choice motivated by my desire to pursue the ministry, for which I was trained and which I love. Besides protecting myself and my vocational options, I believed that I was hiding my sexual orientation for the sake of others—to protect them from knowing something about me that they couldn't handle.

Most people assumed I was a "single" (meaning as-yet-unmarried) heterosexual woman. I did not introduce myself to others that way, but I did conspire in the illusion. I was often asked, "Are you married?" and I answered with a simple "no." The more difficult and just as frequent form of the question was, "Are you single?" I answered that question with a simple "yes," even though I was in a committed relationship with a woman. Each time I answered "yes," I felt a sense of deep betrayal of myself and my relationship.

For years, I believed that secrecy was a necessary evil and my only real choice. I was aware of the costs of coming out. I was less willing to acknowledge the costs of my fear.

I would have thought it strange if someone had suggested that I was exhibiting "internalized homophobia" or that I was collaborating with the norms of a heterosexist society. Then, as now, I accepted myself as lesbian. I was happy in a relationship that I considered not only healthy but grace filled. I just didn't talk about it.

Because not talking about my sexual orientation or my relationship appeared to be my only concession, I fooled myself for years. I denied the way I allowed fear to control my movements, decisions, speech, and relationships with others. The control took many different shapes:

- Although I value truthfulness and openness, my secret meant keeping people at arm's length for fear they might ask uncomfortable questions. I didn't want to have to lie outright.
- I longed to share with others my pride in the human being whom I loved and who loved me. Being unable to share my joy about this most precious gift caused me great pain. At times, I've felt excruciating envy for heterosexual couples who can talk freely about spouses.
- I systematically avoided lesbian sisters and gay brothers, except for a few close friends. At national church events, I did not participate in workshops on lesbian and gay issues or gatherings of the United Church Coalition for Lesbian and Gay Concerns because I feared being seen and identified. I thereby cut myself off from a community of support and nurture that I very much needed.
- Occasionally, in sermons I alluded to justice issues for gay and lesbian people—allusions that were mostly illustrative and quickly passed over as items in a series of other violations of human dignity. I was careful not to speak about lesbian and gay persons as "them" (thereby completely distancing myself), and yet I could not, would not, talk about "us" or "me."

Several events converged, seven or eight years after coming out to myself, that caused me to reconsider my decision to stay in the closet.

I had moved to the Netherlands to be with Christina, a Dutch woman with whom I had fallen in love. As an American in Europe, I was often asked, "Why have you come to the Netherlands, and how long are you staying?" Had my spouse been male, I could have simply answered, "I'm married to a Dutch man." Instead, I told an elaborate story about wanting to do theological study in Europe. I was, indeed, enrolled in a graduate program—that much was true. I'd come to the Netherlands, however, because of my female spouse, and the study had been a *result* of that move rather than its *cause*.

In other words, the story I told, day in and day out for the five years I lived there, wasn't exactly *my* story. Or better said, it was my story with a hole in the middle—a gaping hole. Being unable, or unwilling, to share my joy and delight about my relationship with Christina left another hole, a wound deep inside me.

While serving as the pastor of a Reformed congregation in the Netherlands, I grew increasingly uncomfortable with the discrepancies between what I was preaching and what I was living. Although I had been ordained to preach the good news that fear need not have the last word in our lives, my silence about being lesbian was an unmistakable concession to fear. It was becoming intolerable for me to stand in the pulpit and preach that resurrection and the commonwealth of God can be present-tense realities in our lives when I was unwilling to act on that conviction. It was becoming intolerable for me to encourage people to tell their stories when I was unwilling to tell my own.

I have always believed that my Christian faith and my preaching must address contemporary issues: I spoke out against the placement of cruise missiles on Dutch soil; I condemned the United States' subversion of the Sandinista experiment in Nicaragua; I worked on behalf of refugees seeking sanctuary in the Netherlands. But, for fear of being seen and identified, I avoided contact with lesbian and gay people.

I was serving as a contributing editor for *Sojourners* magazine, writing about the Dutch peace movement and feminism. To that extent I was willing to speak in my own voice—though I silenced myself as a lesbian. In the summer of 1982, I responded to a short article in the magazine that warned of the dangers of the Family Protection Act, which was then before Congress. This act would, among other things, deny gay and lesbian Americans social security benefits. *Sojourners* exposed the act for what it was but also added a qualifying word about homosexuality, making it clear that by condemning the Family Protection Act they were not condoning homosexuality.

I wrote a three-page response, expressing my dismay at the position taken with regard to lesbians and gay men. Speaking of my concern for lesbian and gay "friends" who would hear the message that they were not welcome in the Sojourners Community, I did not have the courage to speak in the first person.

When the July 1985 issue of *Sojourners* arrived, I could no longer avoid the fact that I was in the midst of a crisis. I was outraged and offended by a feature article on sexuality, in which the author suggested that lesbians and gay men within the Christian community have only two "moral" options: to change their sexual orientation or to embrace celibacy. The author had not only impugned my integrity as a Christian who joyfully affirms her sexual orientation but had presumed to call my partnership with a woman "sinful." I wanted to respond to this article and express my shock and outrage. I couldn't bear to write once again in the third person about "lesbians I've known." Yet I wasn't ready to write in the first person, letting the people at *Sojourners* know that the author had been speaking about *me*.

I had to face the fact that I had lost my voice. I could no longer write or speak with integrity without saying "I" or "we." I had alienated myself from my people. I was filled with confusion and shame.

In retrospect, the convergence of these different events proved to be a decisive turning point, a time of *kairos*. I came to understand that I was experiencing a crisis of pronouns, unable to speak or write in the first person. Pronouns are the most telling words in a person's vocabulary: we can distance ourselves by speaking of "them," or we can express identification and solidarity by saying "we."

The most significant decisions often come down to a choice of pronouns. Faith is a personal call, addressed to us by name. We can't answer that call without the pronoun *I*: "Here am *I*." For years, I tried to avoid using pronouns—until I realized that without them we can't tell our own stories or speak in our own voices.

After eight years together, Christina and I separated, and I returned to the United States. I decided that before I entered into a new round of job interviews I needed to find my own voice. And that required a long, hard look at the price that fear had exacted from me. I went into retreat for a year of solitude and reflection, taking with me the writings of women such as Barbara Deming, Carter Heyward, Adrienne Rich, and Audre Lorde. I tried to identify and name the messages and the threats that fear so long had whispered in my ear.

I discovered that fear's fundamental message to me was: "Whatever you do, Melanie, DON'T TALK ABOUT IT. Don't talk about the fact that you are lesbian." This warning was spoken by friends who genuinely believed they were looking out for my well-being. I often repeated it to myself. In a heterosexist society, the worst offense a lesbian or gay person can commit is to be "self-avowed" and proud. Talking openly is seen as disruptive, flaunting, distracting, and indelicate. The "don't talk about it" messages take many forms:

- Don't talk about it, because it will cause you to lose your credibility.
- Don't talk about it, because people will label you and write you off. They will know you as the "lesbian minister." (Why aren't others identified as "heterosexual ministers"?)
- Don't talk about it, because you'll be seen as a single-issue person. You'll lose your authority to talk about other important matters.
- Don't talk about it, because you won't be able to work in the church. Even members of a congregation who

presume that you are lesbian may not mind as long as you don't "flaunt it" by talking about it.
• Don't talk about it, because it's no one else's business anyway. It's a private matter, a bedroom issue. Heterosexual people don't feel it necessary to talk about their private lives in job interviews.

To counter these messages, I had to learn to speak in my own voice. I'm still learning, but I've begun to talk back.

Even if I were to lose all credibility and not be allowed to address any other matter, is anything more important than this? This is *my* oppression, and it has everything to do with other forms of oppression.

If I'm seen by others as a single-issue person, the problem lies in their perception. I know that I'm not a single-issue person.

To speak openly about who I am and the person I love is not flaunting. Heterosexual people talk freely about who they went out with last weekend and who they find attractive. They wear wedding rings and proudly show pictures of their spouses. They embrace and hold hands in public places. If my partner and I do any of these things, people look askance and ask: "Maybe they can't help who they are, but why do they have to flaunt it?"

To say that I am a lesbian isn't a purely private matter. It isn't a bedroom issue. To say that I am a lesbian sets me free to build community and express solidarity with sisters and brothers, reaching out to individuals and families who live isolated lives for fear that sharing their secret will bring reproach and rejection. To say that I am a lesbian is to join with others to work against our oppression and to say clearly that I believe in the gospel which liberates us from fear. It involves recognizing and using the gifts I have to offer others and the church not in spite of, but by virtue of, being a lesbian in this society.

During that year of solitude, wrestling with the demon of fear, I realized that I had to come out to any future search committee. For I can't tell my story and account for my life choices without saying that I am a lesbian. I can't explain why I live here rather than there, why I'm doing the work I am doing, and why I love the person I love without talking about my sexual orientation. I can't say what the Christian faith means to me, who Jesus and God are for me, and what the scriptural stories say to me, without revealing my life context of oppression and liberation as a lesbian.

When I decided to remain silent no longer, doors slammed behind me—vocational doors and doors to some relationships with friends. I felt I might be swallowed up by fear.

That has not happened.

I've learned real-life lessons about the meaning and the power of resurrection. I've learned that life can't be shut up in the grave (or the closet) unless we allow it to remain there. Neither death nor its first cousin, fear, needs to have the last word.

Some doors closed, but others have opened. Because I've risked visibility, other people have felt free to share their stories with me. We can now support and hold up hope to one another. Each time I see human beings turn from self-hatred and fear toward the conviction that they, too, as lesbian or gay persons, are beloved children of God, I witness grace at work. I've been blessed with the love of friends, family, and strangers who accept me as I am. I've found wonderfully diverse communities of lesbian sisters and gay brothers.

The costs of coming out are real—some doors remain closed. Each of us must weigh these costs and roll away the stone of secrecy only when she or he is ready. I can only testify that the freedom I now know far outweighs the costs. When I am able to act on the conviction that not rejection, hatred, rupture of friendships, loss of a job, or threatened violence can separate me from the love of God, I know once again that resurrection is real.

3

SINGING HOPE'S SONG

IN A STRANGE LAND

By the rivers of Babylon—
there we sat down and there
    we wept
when we remembered Zion.
On the willows there
    we hung up our harps.
For there our captors
    asked us for songs,
and our tormentors asked for
    mirth, saying,
"Sing us one of the songs of Zion!"
How could we sing God's song in a foreign land?
If I forget you, O Jerusalem,
    let my right hand wither!
Let my tongue cling to the roof of   .
    my mouth,
if I do not remember you . . .
          —PSALM 137

My friend Toni met me for coffee shortly after the 1994 congressional election. Candidates promising a conservative social and political agenda were elected in record numbers. The numbness and shock from November 8 were wearing off, but it was still diffi-

This is an Advent meditation written after the November 1994 elections.

14

cult to say out loud how afraid we were for ourselves and for this country.

"Sometimes I feel like I live on another planet," Toni said, "because the things I care so passionately about don't seem to matter to most people I come in contact with."

I nodded, remembering some of the campaign slogans that had most disturbed me. "It's sort of like being an exile in one's own country, isn't it?"

I am wary of using certain words as spiritual metaphors. "Exile" is one of those words. Those of us who have never known the excruciating pain of being forcibly separated from our native land should beware of spiritualizing the experience and appropriating the term. Millions of people at this historical moment are exiled from their homelands for political and economic reasons.

Thus, I did not make my remark casually. I was echoing her experience of feeling profoundly out of sync or at odds with many of the citizens of our own country. Different ones of us have known this condition of feeling like exiles in our own country: because our sexual orientation brands us as outsiders; because our values clash with the values of the dominant culture; because the world we so passionately yearn for doesn't seem to be the world that those around us want.

In 597 B.C.E., the Babylonians invaded Judah, ransacked Jerusalem, burned the temple, and sent the Jewish leaders into exile in Babylonia. The Babylonian captivity lasted seventy years.

Psalm 137 reflects the unmitigated pain of being in exile. The people sit down and weep as they remember their homeland. They hang their harps on the willows by the river. They are too heartbroken to sing. Their captors had mocked and goaded them, saying, "Come on, sing one of those songs from the old country!"

The people ask, "How can we sing God's song in a foreign land?" It is too painful. Singing of their homeland stirs up too many memories and longings that can't be met. They are tempted to forget. But then, the psalmist declares, "I must never forget, never."

Centuries later, the refusal to be numbed against pain and to retire from the struggle is echoed in the words of poet Adrienne Rich:

. . . no person, trying to take responsibility for her or his identity, should have to be so alone. There must be those among whom we can sit down and weep, and still be counted as warriors . . . we who want an end to suffering, who want to change the laws of history, if we are not to give ourselves away.

. . . I have wished I could rest among the beautiful and common weeds I can name, both here and in other tracts of the globe. But there is no finite knowing, no such rest. Innocent birds, deserts, morning-glories, point to choices, leading away from the familiar. When I speak of an end to suffering I don't mean anesthesia. I mean knowing the world, and my place in it, not in order to stare with bitterness or detachment, but as a powerful and womanly series of choices.[1]

In this post-election Advent season, I feel tossed between the temptation to retreat in cynicism and the recognition that I still possess a powerful and womanly series of choices. The purported election "mandate" is so devoid of vision and so full of fear and despair. It is a spiritual challenge to resist falling into the deep well of despair that threatens our nation. The flame of hope has only been a faint flicker in me in the weeks since the election. The denial mechanisms and defenses that usually shield me have been malfunctioning. I am frightened.

I am frightened by our failure to reach consensus on the urgency of health care reform, an issue that affects all of us in the United States.
I am frightened by the ascendancy of economic policies that promise to assist the upper classes by slashing programs for those most vulnerable and marginalized.
I am frightened by the fact that "entitlement" is a dirty word in the minds of so many Americans.
I am frightened by the backlash of angry white men.
I am frightened by the fact that building more prisons seems to be the only unified response we can make to crime.

I am frightened by how often Americans' rage is dis-
placed onto vulnerable scapegoats like poor, teenaged
mothers.
I am frightened by the fact that every new Republican
member of Congress was required to sit through lectures
at the Heritage Foundation by such people as Rush
Limbaugh.
I am frightened by the militant heterosexist agenda of the
Christian Coalition.
I am frightened by the insistence of one newly elected
member of Congress that this election boiled down to
three things: "God, gays, and guns." As he put it, "We
want God in our schools, we want gays out of the mili-
tary, and we want our guns back."
I am frightened by the news that one of the fastest growing organizations in the state of Michigan is The Militia,
a paramilitary force that opposes gun control and U.S. in-
volvement in the United Nations.

Those are only some the things of which I am afraid and some of the
reasons why I feel like an exile in my own country.

Another reason for my sense of exile concerns the season of
Advent. Because an advent hope is rooted in an unquenchable and
passionate yearning for a world transformed, an advent faith will not
allow me to rest in the way things are—it points me "to choices,
leading away from the familiar." I cannot settle for the new world
order of advanced capitalism, which means good news for the rich
and bad news for the poor. An advent faith points me to the new
order of the Spirit about which Mary sang, a time when the mighty
will be brought low and the poor lifted up.

I have been consciously calling to mind, along with the fearful
realities that I named earlier, memories of Advent from years past. As
April and I search for Advent rituals that can authentically reflect our
values and our different styles of believing, I have been telling her
about some ways my family observed and celebrated Advent. In this
post-election time, this exercise of remembering has made me aware
that my life is rooted in another calendar, in other, more compelling,

seasons. Like Advent—a time of waiting, pregnant with hope. Despite my fear and the temptation to despair, I have recovered memories of wonder, awe, anticipation, and mystery.

In my family's observance of Advent and Christmas, I heard the message—through all the commercial interference—that Christmas was about the birth of love. I sensed that Christmas had something to do with my father and mother's tireless work in the 1950s for an open-occupancy ordinance to end the racist policies of realtors in East Lansing. I knew that Christmas had something to do with the work that caused my parents to get anonymous letters calling them communists. I knew that Christmas had to do with my father's exile from his southern homeland after his understanding of the Christian faith had caused him to vocally object when he witnessed racist incidents. I knew that Christmas had to do with my mother walking from house to house during Advent fifty years ago, urging people to sign a petition supporting the establishment of something called the United Nations.

As I grew older, I more clearly understood Christmas as being central to a faith and a world view which declared that bodies matter and that every child's life is sacred. I understood faith as a commitment to persevere in the struggle for justice, refusing to rest until the advent of a new world, continuing to believe as though our lives depended upon it (and they do!) that the future is not closed but open. The angels and shepherds and the star are magical, but theirs is not the magic of fairy tales. Rather it is the hope-giving mystery that stirs us to believe again that the things we see around us—the things that often bid for our allegiance and attention, energy, time, and money—are not the things that truly matter. Those angels and shepherds and that star were ancient messengers announcing that God intends a different world and that the future is open because there is a light that shines in the midst of fear, a light that the fear has never overcome.

It is this advent hope that most profoundly makes me an exile in my own country. The faith I inherited and the hope I affirm set me squarely at odds with much of American culture. But life at the margins can be a place of ferment and creativity, a place in which to discover a sustained urgency to imagine new structures, new ways of relating, new forms of speech.

It is more imperative than ever—in the midst of these frightening times—that we nurture communities where we can dream and laugh together, where we can sit down and weep and "still be counted as warriors," where we can know the world as it is and our place in it, where we can face the choices we need to make, where we can actively care for each other, where we can keep hope alive by celebrating even the smallest victories and joys, where we can sing hope's song in a strange land.

In this Advent season, we can find the strength to sing our heart's desire when we remember that the dreaming, the nurturing, the weeping, and the singing are not accomplished by our efforts alone. A Spirit, a holy presence, is coming to birth among us, to dwell with us and to accompany us. Despite all the evidence to the contrary, the future is open. It is open because the holy presence at the heart of the universe will journey with us in our exile until we arrive at our true homeland—where no one will be considered a stranger, where no one will suffer abuse or hunger, and where all will be welcomed and called beloved.

4

THE HEART OF
THE MATTER

I was invited to spend a few days with a Christian community that I had had some acquaintance with, and great respect for, over the years. The community consists of about thirty men, women, and children who live on a couple hundred acres of land. They live simply, sharing all things in common and giving shelter and other assistance to all those in need. These people asked me to come meet with them and lead them through two days of study and discussion.

The question they were wrestling with was whether a lesbian or gay couple could become residents of the community. Although they insisted that everyone was welcome in their community, the controversy revolved around the question of whether prospective gay and lesbian community members would have to remain celibate in order to conform to the community's stated policy that sexual expression was to be limited to (heterosexual) marriage.

We had very intensive days together: honest, confessional, and confrontational. There were tears at times. I saw people struggling against the full weight of inherited assumptions about the Bible, about what is natural and unnatural, and about what God wills for human sexuality. They had asked me to facilitate the sessions because I am lesbian, because I do that kind of work for a living, and because of my tie with their community. It was a very poignant experience of what Marilyn Frye calls the experience of being both insider and outsider, friend and stranger, member of the family and exile.[1]

Perhaps because I had lived in such a community in the days when I thought I was heterosexual, I had a keen sense of heterosexual privilege. I saw these heterosexual couples expressing affection openly, wearing their wedding rings, having babies, living in their houses, building their families, talking about their relationships. No one questioned the rightness or wrongness of their being together. But there we were, gathered for study and prayer and intense discussion about my life, my family, my love, and the lives, families, and loves of my lesbian sisters and gay brothers.

At times, my ability to absorb the "problem" broke down and I wondered how these people who loved and respected me could fail to rejoice with me that I am blessed in my partnership with April. There were times when I wanted to set aside my professional demeanor and shout, "Who appointed you the gatekeepers? Who made you the judges? What gives you the right to even think that you can approve or disapprove of my life and my love?" I didn't shout. But I did speak boldly, directly, and passionately.

At one point, a community member explained that neither he nor others there were biblical literalists or fundamentalists. "What I really want to know," he said, "is what Jesus might say to us. I want to live in accord with the spirit of Christ in this as in all matters."

I told him that, contrary to popular assumptions, the gospels have no record of words spoken by Jesus about homosexuality. Not one condemning word. Nevertheless, we *can* ask how Jesus might respond to homosexuality. We can draw analogies from how he taught and lived and responded to other subjects. Jesus also had much to say about the scriptures, how to interpret them and how to discern when they are being rightfully and wrongfully used. Jesus radically reinterpreted the scriptures—particularly those that were used as justification for excluding some people from the community. He redefined the boundaries of who was in and who was out. When he pushed against accepted boundaries, he was accused of violating God's word in scripture.

One part of the scriptures that Jesus radically reinterpreted was the purity codes found in Leviticus (chaps. 11–16 and 17–26). Central to all the purity codes was the command that the people of Israel be holy as God is holy. Two passages most frequently cited by those who contend that the Bible and God condemn homosexuality are found in the purity codes (Lev. 18:22 and 20:13).

Jesus did not specifically address the passages in Leviticus that speak of same-gender sexual behaviors; but by way of analogy, he gave us guidelines for how they might be interpreted. Leviticus contains elaborate provisions for setting apart those rendered unclean by virtue of leprosy. The purity codes state that lepers must wear torn clothing and disheveled hair, and when anyone approaches they must shout, "unclean, unclean!" They are to live alone, outside the community. If a person with leprosy is healed, there are elaborate rituals of cleansing, and until the person undergoes those rituals under the guidance of a priest, the person is not restored to full participation in the community.

Leviticus states that a menstruating woman is to be considered unclean—as well as anyone who touches her. There are prohibitions against people with disabilities being ordained to the priesthood. And there are laws that prohibit the eating of certain foods because they are unclean or the sacrifice of certain animals because they are blemished.

The concern with holiness and purity in Leviticus has to do, first and foremost, with what can and cannot be brought to the Temple and who may and may not approach the Temple. According to the authors of Leviticus, holiness is related to "wholeness and completion" in creation.[2] Therefore, the purity codes stipulate that only those people, animals, and other created things that approach physical perfection meet the standards of holiness that the Temple requires. Holiness, according to the authors of Leviticus, also forbids the mixing or confusion of different created classes of things. Therefore, the cross breeding of cattle or the creation of hybrids by mixing two kinds of seeds was considered an abomination. Levitical rules of sexual morality also defined as "impure" that which does not conform fully to its class. Anthropologist Mary Douglas summarizes the Levitical understanding of holiness in this way:

> We can conclude that holiness is exemplified by completeness. Holiness requires that individuals shall conform to the class to which they belong. And holiness requires that different classes of things shall not be confused . . . Holiness means keeping distinct the categories of creation.[3]

How did Jesus observe the purity codes? He approached them as he approached everything, carrying with him the conviction that God's love is radically inclusive and that sin is the exclusion of some from the rest.[4] He carried with him the guiding interpretive principles which he believed formed the heart of the scriptures: namely, that we are to love God with all our heart, mind, and soul and we are to love our neighbors as ourselves. Jesus redefined purity and impurity, claiming that physical purity is not the truest measure of holiness. Holiness has, instead, to do with purity of heart and purity of heart is determined by adherence to the "weightier matters" of the law: justice and mercy and faith (Matt. 23:23).

Jesus observed what he believed to be the heart of the scriptures by touching lepers and being touched by them. He restored them to health, dignity, and human community not by rituals of cleansing but by reaching out and welcoming in, by touching and restoring relationship. In that radical act of touching he said, in effect, "those whom God has declared clean, we must not declare unclean."

When Jesus was touched by a hemorrhaging woman, he didn't reprimand her for making him unclean; rather, he commended her act of faith in reaching out to touch and be touched. He ate with people who are labeled unclean and sinners. He ate and healed on the Sabbath, making some people very angry by seeming to violate the scriptures. When confronted with this charge he said, "I have not come to do away with the scriptures or the law, but to fulfill them." He said in effect, "Love and justice are the central moral norms—the heart of the matter—and the scriptures are fulfilled whenever and wherever love and justice are done."

Shortly after Jesus' death, the inclusivity of the new Christian church was confronted by its first test case. The controversy concerned Philip's baptism of an Ethiopian eunuch. Some people were outraged that Philip had violated the scriptures and tradition by baptizing someone considered to be sexually abnormal and outside the faith community. Philip's opponents objected that this baptism was in clear violation of the scriptures. His defense was that he had acted in the spirit of Christ: this Ethiopian eunuch, he said, loved God and desired to live a just and faithful life. That was the heart of the matter, Philip argued.

The book of Acts also tells how Peter, a leader in the early Christian church, was convinced that Gentiles needed to be circumcised before they could be baptized. Peter's tradition and scriptures had taught him that uncircumcised Gentiles were unclean. But in a dream, Peter heard a heavenly voice putting this question to him, "Peter, what God has called clean, do you dare call unclean?" So Peter baptized the uncircumcised Gentiles, and when he was called by the church elders to defend his actions he said, "If God wishes to give them the same gift that God gave us, who am I to stand in the way of the Spirit of God?"

The drama and confrontation that we hear in this story about Peter, in the controversy around the baptism of the eunuch, and in the controversies that surrounded Jesus wherever he went, are the same drama and confrontation we hear today. Some people insist that the scriptures be literally obeyed, word for word, without picking and choosing. Others insist that all of us, even the most fundamentalist Christians, engage in some form of selection.

There are those who invoke scripture to deny lesbians and gay men justice and full participation in synagogue and church. And there are those who invoke the spirit behind and within the scriptures as inspiration in the struggle for justice and full inclusion for lesbians and gay men. The drama and confrontation revolve around how one understands the heart of the matter.

By what measure can we then discern the heart of the matter? It seems to me that the measure Jesus used was that the scriptures must never be placed above persons, nor may they be used to justify human prejudice. Jesus was committed to setting aside every religious tradition or interpretation of scripture that violated "the oneness of God and the oneness of God's human community."[5] If any of us tries to argue that love or justice should be withheld and we base that argument on scripture, I believe Jesus would urge us to take another good, hard look at our interpretation.

During the study and discussion sessions in the community, people said that they longed to do the right and faithful thing, believing they will one day have to stand before God and account for their actions. They said that they could not, in good conscience, affirm something that might be morally wrong.

I could hear their earnestness. These community members were honestly wrestling with all of this. And I said to them, "It is indeed a serious thing to call that which is wrong, good; that which is sinful, right. However, when I read the Gospels, I hear Jesus saying that it is an equally serious thing, if not more serious, to call that which is good, sinful; that which is clean, unclean; that which is right, wrong. You and I will also have to answer to the Creator for such judgments."

I also shared with them something that had happened to me not long before. I was speaking to a college class about my experience as a lesbian and a pastor, and one of the women in the class said, "Well, I have to tell you that even though I find you a likable person, I can't condone what you are doing. I think it's a sin. But, I can still love you. It's possible to love the sinner and hate the sin."

"How can you say that you love me," I responded, "when you don't want to know either my pain or my joy? No, I don't think you can say that you love me, because what you call 'sin' (the love I share with April), I call a grace-filled relationship, and what you call your inability to condone, I call the sin of heterosexism. There's a serious rupture between us, and we can't gloss it over with easy talk about loving the sinner while hating the sin. For you to call the most intimate and cherished relationship in my life 'sinful' is a very serious charge. It's a violent thing to say. Furthermore, you can't offer me love with one hand while denying me justice with the other, because love and justice are inseparable. No, I'm sorry, I won't grant you your wish to think that you can love me anyway."

I told the people of this Christian community that story because some of them genuinely could not understand why the insistence on celibacy was, to me, the same as rejection. "But we affirm you, we love you," they insisted. "We just may not be able to affirm your behavior."

I tried to impress upon them that they could not split me into pieces that way. The love that Jesus embodied is a love that makes whole, that sets free, that rejoices in liberation and healing. Coming home to myself as a lesbian has been profoundly healing. Coming out to others and overcoming fear are profoundly liberating. Finding love like the love I share with April is an experience of grace.

In the gospel stories, when people are healed, when people find love and acceptance and community, frequently someone steps forward and says to Jesus, "But that person who touched you is unclean and the scriptures say you must not touch her!" Or they step forward and say, "Why are you healing on the Sabbath? That is against the scriptures." When scripture is quoted to Jesus in that fashion, he is saddened and angry. He says things like, "Ought not this woman, a daughter of Abraham whom Satan bound for eighteen long years, be set free from this bondage on the Sabbath Day?"

As I listen to Jesus, I hear him saying that it is a very serious thing to declare unclean what God has declared clean, to place outside the community those whom God would welcome in. I hear him saying that it is tragic, if not sinful, to be unable to rejoice with those who have found love and wholeness and healing. I hear him saying that using scripture to defend injustice or to withhold love is wrongheaded interpretation which has missed the heart of the matter.

God's love is radically inclusive, and God will not be bound by human barriers or prejudice. God will do the calling and the welcoming. The heart of the matter is not our sexual orientation; the heart of the matter is how we live our lives, whatever our sexual orientation. The heart of the matter is, as another prophet summed it up, to act justly, to love tenderly, and to walk reverently with the Creator.

5

You Are My Beloved

Toni Morrison's mesmerizing novel *Beloved* is set in post-Civil War Ohio. It is the story of Sethe, an escaped slave who has lost her husband, buried a child, been raped, and been whipped so badly her back has no feeling in it, only scars in the shape of a tree. She has seen and borne unthinkable suffering and somehow not gone mad.

Sethe lives a reclusive life with her daughter, Denver, and her mother-in-law, Baby Suggs. Their house is haunted by the ghost of Beloved, a child Sethe killed in infancy in order to spare her the dehumanization and suffering of slavery.

The novel's epigraph quotes the ninth chapter of Paul's letter to the Romans: "I will call them my people, which were not my people; and her beloved, which was not beloved." The apostle Paul was writing about redemption and so was Toni Morrison. She dedicated *Beloved* to the "Sixty Million and More"—the estimated number of Africans and African Americans who died as a result of slavery. Morrison said in an interview that she expected this novel to be her least read novel because "it is about something that the characters don't want to remember, black people don't want to remember, white people don't want to remember. I mean, it's national amnesia . . ."[1]

The ghost of the slain child, Beloved, is the tangible presence of a past that initially had to be escaped and repressed by the former

This sermon was preached on the occasion of Julian Richard Day Cooney's baptism.

slaves as they struggled to survive. The novel suggests, however, that unless the painful past can be recovered, ancestral ghosts will haunt succeeding generations: "The invasion of the world of the living by Beloved's physical presence is evidence of the terrible destruction of the natural order caused by slavery."[2]

Redemption occurs for the people in this novel as they remember the brutality and horror of slavery while also "recovering what is lost and loving it into life."[3] The characters in *Beloved* are not larger than life—not heroes or villains. They hurt and disappoint each other. They also love and pull each other through circumstances that could have crushed them, body and soul.

Toward the end of the novel, thirty neighborhood women gather to exorcise Beloved's ghost and free Sethe from the insatiable guilt that has consumed her. Their act of love and solidarity is described with baptismal imagery as a ritual of healing and rebirth. The women surround Sethe with song, their voices searching "for the right combination, the key, the code, the sound that broke the back of words. Building voice upon voice until they found it, and when they did it was a wave of sound wide enough to sound deep water and knock the pods off chestnut trees. It broke over Sethe and she trembled like the baptized in its wash."[4]

Shortly after this climactic event, Sethe's lover, Paul D., returns after being gone for several months. He finds Sethe in bed, "lying under a quilt of merry colors," where she has been for days. Afraid that Sethe is planning to die, he tenderly tries to coax her out of bed and he assures her that he is back to care for her. Sethe says:

> *"[Beloved] left me."*
> *"Aw, girl. Don't cry."*
> *"She was my best thing."* . . .
> *"Sethe," [Paul D.] says, "me and you, we got more yesterday than anybody. We need some kind of tomorrow."*
> *He leans over and takes her hand. With the other he touches her face. "You your best thing, Sethe. You are." His holding fingers are holding hers.*
> *"Me? Me?"*[5]

In the scene that Matthew paints for us of Jesus' baptism, the heavens open; the Spirit, like a dove, rests on Jesus; and a voice is heard saying, "This is my beloved Son, with whom I am well pleased." For years, when I heard that story, I found it somewhat magical—with the heavens opening, a dove descending, and a disembodied voice speaking. I assumed God's words were addressed to Jesus and Jesus only. Then, my friend and copastor Cyril Colonius preached a Father's Day sermon entitled "The Wounded Father." Cyril talked about his troubled, conflicted relationship with his father, "You know, all my life, I have been waiting to hear those words from my father: 'This is my beloved Son, with whom I am well pleased.'"

When Cyril said this, I realized that all of us are waiting, yearning, aching to hear the words, "you are my beloved with whom I am well pleased." We are waiting, yearning, aching to hear, "you are your own best thing." That is the heart of the good news that Jesus would have us hear. That is what we proclaim when we baptize Julian today: "He is a beloved child with whom God is well pleased."

While living in the Netherlands, I heard a story about a seven-year-old who was dressing up and looking at himself in the mirror. Delighted with what he saw, he ran into the kitchen where his mother was busily preparing supper. "Look at me, Mom!" he shouted. His mother was too distracted at first to even respond, so he tugged at her, "Look, Mom, look how beautiful I am!" His mother glanced in his direction but didn't really focus on him. She nodded perfunctorily, "Uh huh, I see."

"No, you don't, you don't!" he said angrily, "You don't see me."

"I *do*," she protested without looking up from the stove.

Then the little boy said, "I wish you could look at me through my eyes so you could see how beautiful I am."

This little boy's need to be seen is what psychologists call healthy narcissism—a developmental stage they say is vitally important, especially in infancy. In that stage, a child needs to see a parent's face bending over a crib and to hear the words, "You are my precious one. You are so beautiful. There is no one as beautiful in all the world!"

We know that Julian Richard Day Cooney will not be deprived of this message or this developmental stage. He will not grow up wishing he could hear his father and his mother say, "You are my beloved." Julian is also blessed with a wider faith community that will tell him in all kinds of ways about God's passionate desire to be humanity's loving companion. He will hear and learn that passion is at the heart of the universe; that from this divine passion is born our human yearning for connection, our delight in bodies and sexual touch, and our hunger for justice.

Unfortunately, there is a theology of baptism and a christology that would try to convince Julian that appropriating the words, "You are my beloved with whom I am well pleased" is blasphemous and arrogant—that these words were intended only for Jesus. Because he alone is sinless. He is everything that we are not. This theology insists that we are fundamentally unworthy, not pleasing in God's sight, and that our redemption must be purchased at a terrible cost. These baptismal waters are a means of washing us of our sins. Even one so tiny as Julian, it is said, is already tainted by birth into this fallen world.

That theology and christology have molded an understanding of baptism that breeds fear, shame, and self-contempt—particularly about our bodies and sexuality. Inherent in this understanding of baptism is a false equation: that we must decrease so that Jesus may increase. We learn this false equation as children when we sing the last line of "Jesus Loves Me" . . . I am weak but he is strong.

We want children to hear that Jesus loves them. We want children to know that they are seen with eyes that find them beautiful, cherished, brightly shining persons. We may even want them to hear that when they're feeling weak, they can lean on Jesus. But I fear if children learn the words, "we are weak but he is strong," they don't hear that *they* are beloved. Instead they hear, "Jesus is good. Jesus is special. Jesus is strong. Jesus is a lover . . . not me, not you."

A Jewish story tells about a wise man, Reb Elimelech, who cannot understand why people follow his carriage throughout the town. Elimelech asks his coachman why all these people are trailing behind the carriage. The coachman explains that the people are seeking wisdom and holiness. Elimelech decides that they are doing the right thing, so he gets out of the carriage and disappears into the procession, joining the people who now follow an empty carriage.[6]

When I'm weak, God makes me strong?

I believe that Jesus of Nazareth—the anointed one—wants us to know that God is with us as we work, love, speak, decide, struggle, and seek to keep God's dream for creation alive. God is with us, but neither God nor Jesus will do our working, loving, speaking, deciding, struggling, or dreaming for us. I believe that Jesus wants Julian to grow up to affirm who he is: a beloved child of God, a person both blessed and accountable, a person called to live his life with reverence and responsibility. I believe that any affirmation of Jesus that would cancel Julian out would deeply grieve Jesus. I believe that Jesus long ago got out of the carriage and joined us in the search for holiness and wisdom.

Without being naive about the human capacity for evil, self-deception, and self-righteousness, Jesus longed to have every person hear that he or she is beloved. For Jesus was love made flesh: love that is seeringly honest not sentimental; love that is passionate; love that feels and expresses rage at injustice; love is that grieved by both self-righteousness and self-contempt; love that is rooted in the knowledge and experience of forgiveness. Jesus taught that those people who are incapable of really loving are the same people who have never felt the need to be forgiven. But those who have experienced being welcomed home, held, and accepted, precisely when they believed they were unacceptable—those are the people who know love and who know how to love. Jesus said it this way: those who have been forgiven much love much. John addressed the early community that gathered in Jesus' name as "beloved": "Beloved, let us love one another, for love is of God, and those who love are born of God and know God. Beloved, if God so loved us, we also ought to love one another."

Baptism proclaims a mystery: that nothing, absolutely nothing we do or are, can separate Julian or any one of us from this love of God in Christ. It is mysterious, almost unfathomable, such love, especially knowing what we do about our lives. That God should find Julian precious and beloved is not difficult to grasp. His spontaneity, single-heartedness, and vulnerability are surely pleasing in God's sight. But with those of us who are gathered here today as his community—with us it is more difficult to grasp, knowing what we do about our lives. By the time Julian is old enough to understand

atonement = at-one-ment
Silence is a cousin of fear

the words that have been spoken today and the symbols of this sacrament, he will also be old enough to doubt. He will have to make his own decision for or against his baptism, for or against this outrageous love. If he chooses against it, he will have every proof that reason and the evidence of this broken world can muster. If he chooses for it, he will live from faith. He is free, as each of us here today is free, to do what he will with this baptism. But not Julian, nor you, nor I can ever alter what it means: that we were created in love for love; that God would have us hear, "You are my beloved, you are your own best thing."

6

CREATING NEW RITUALS

RITES OF PASSAGE IN LESBIAN AND GAY COMMUNITIES

Lesbians and gay men are often referred to as if we are part of one subculture or one movement. Common parlance not withstanding, there is no such thing as *the* lesbian community or *the* gay community, much less *the* lesbian *and* gay community. Lesbians and gay men are found in every ethnic group; we are part of many cultures, many ethnicities, many classes, and many races. This diversity is reflected in many different kinds of rituals being created in different lesbian and gay communities.

I write from the context of being a white, middle-class ordained minister who finds herself by choice and relegation on the margins of the Christian church and tradition. By virtue of my gender and my sexual orientation, I am relegated to the margins; by virtue of my lesbian feminist liberation perspective, I choose to be on the margins. I will discuss primarily those rituals with which I am personally familiar; rituals being created by lesbians and gay men whose religious heritage is Christian. A Wiccan lesbian, a Jewish lesbian, or a lesbian identified with the recovery of goddess rituals would have different illustrations and anecdotes. While occasionally referring to some of those different traditions, I speak from the only context from which I can speak—my own.

In his study of Western Europe from the beginning of the Christian era to the fourteenth century, historian John Boswell documents parallels between the discrimination and violence directed against Jews and the discrimination and violence directed against gay men and lesbians. His research shows that Jews and gay people have shared a common lot throughout European history. Their enemies were frequently the same groups, and intolerance for Jewish distinctiveness went hand in hand with violence against sexual nonconformity.[1] Boswell documents how similar methods of propaganda were employed against both minority groups, "portraying them as animals bent on the destruction of the children of the majority."[2]

Boswell notes that Jews, unlike gay men and lesbians, are born into families that impart stories about past violence, that warn of present dangers, and that offer community and solidarity in the face of oppression. Jewish children are taught early about the reality of anti-Semitism and about their people's survival, often against great odds. A body of sacred and secular literature transmits the stories of the Jewish people, and liturgical commemorations recall the suffering and celebrate survival and hope. Gay men and lesbians, however, are not, for the most part, born into families with gay or lesbian parents and grandparents. Boswell points out that gay people

> *suffer oppression individually and alone, without benefit of advice or frequently even emotional support from relatives or friends. . . . When good times return there is no mechanism to encourage steps to prevent a recurrence of oppression: no gay grandparents who remember the pogroms, no gay exile literature to remind the living of the fate of the dead, no liturgical commemorations in times of suffering and crisis.*[3]

While I find Boswell's thesis illuminating, I think it is only partially accurate. It is certainly the case that most of us who are lesbian or gay have few biological forebears to warn us of the dangers and pass on the stories of hope and survival. But we no longer lack exile literature to remind the living of the fate of the dead. Nor are we without liturgical commemorations in times of suffering and crisis.

Although the biological family unit is not the conduit by which traditions are passed from generation to generation within lesbian and gay communities, traditions nevertheless are being passed. Songs, poems, novels, and essays are being written, and life passages are being celebrated. This body of literature and these rituals are crucially important, precisely because we are a minority without biological minority families.

Philosopher Marilyn Frye has noted that the status of being both "citizen and exile, member of the family and stranger" can function as a blessing. Because lesbians and gay men know the straight world from the inside and the outside, we possess a different way of seeing and envisioning:

> We can look at [the straight world] with the accuracy and depth provided by binocular vision. With the knowledge available to us from our different perches at the margins of things, we can base our inventions of ourselves, inventions of what a woman is and what a man is, on a really remarkable understanding of humans and human society as they have been constructed and misconstructed before.[4]

Frye reminds us that the powers to look with accuracy and depth at societal norms and traditions and to break with dominant norms and invent new ones have to do with social location. Marginality, difference, and deviance (when chosen and claimed) contain, as Frye says, "healing and revelatory power." The key ingredient here is *choice*.

> For the benefits of marginality to be reaped, marginality must in some sense be chosen. . . . One cannot see what is to be seen from one's particular vantage point or know what can be known to a body so located if one is preoccupied with wishing one were not there, denying the peculiarity of one's position, disowning oneself.[5]

Recently I visited a traveling exhibition of photography, art work, and artifacts, called Rites of Passage in America: Traditions of the Life Cycle. This exhibition portrayed the ways in which Americans from nineteen different ethnic backgrounds celebrate four major life passages: birth, coming of age, marriage, and death. I was delighted to see that the exhibition included illustrations of how life passages in lesbian and gay communities are celebrated. Amidst displays showing a Latino money dance, a Croatian wedding, and turn-of-the-century immigrant trousseaus, was a window case featuring the lesbian union of an African American woman and a Jewish woman, replete with a photograph of the couple and wedding symbols from both of their cultures. Artifacts chosen to reflect traditions surrounding the final passage of death also included photographs of the AIDS quilt.

Walking through the exhibit, I felt keenly, poignantly, what it is to be both citizen and exile, member of the family and stranger. My lesbian sisters and gay brothers are present throughout the exhibition—not just in the window case labeled lesbian and gay— many standing unrecognized, unknown, in the photographs, presumed to be heterosexual. We are represented within all the cultures in the exhibition: Native American, Ukrainian American, Asian American, and African American (to name but a few). And in each of these cultures, we are—to a lesser or greater extent—both citizen and exile, member of the family and stranger.

Many lesbian or gay adults remember the pain of feeling coerced to participate in the heterosexual rites of passage the exhibition portrayed. Because the dominant culture and most ethnic subcultures have no coming-of-age rituals that recognize a sexual minority in their midst, we attempted to navigate the harrowing waters of adolescence and young adulthood, trying to be straight, imitating our peers' desire for the opposite sex, and hiding— sometimes from ourselves, always from others—an inescapable sense of being aliens, off balance, out of sync. On prom night, some of us got sick and had an excuse not to attend; others, mercifully, were never invited; and a few attended with a same-sex date, enduring stares, insults, ridicule, or media sensationalism.

A good number of us married people of the other sex, in opposition to what our bodies, desires, and dreams were telling us. The memory of that particular rite of passage is an excruciating memory of being profoundly split. We desperately wanted to feel the happiness that everyone was wishing us, but we stood outside our bodies, watching ourselves dance and laugh and participate in the rituals.

Some of us have had to endure the funeral of a lover, in which we never heard our name or the relationship named by the person officiating. We were labeled euphemistically as "friend" by hospital personnel, family members, and clergy, and we were not consulted about the funeral plans. The obituary did not mention that the deceased had been living in a partnership, perhaps for years. We sat in the midst of mourners unknown and unseen.

We were—especially at such closeted moments—citizens and exiles, members of the family and strangers, possessing dual vision but not yet able to claim it as power; not yet able to claim the true location of our lesbian and gay bodyselves. Not yet able to see from our particular vantage point with accuracy and depth. The violence and violation experienced by closeted lesbians and gay men during such rites of passage are indescribable.

As we come out in increasing numbers, claiming the power of our location and our binocular vision, increasingly we are inventing rituals and rites of passage that cohere with our lives. We are choosing our own language, symbols, images, and music to create rituals for our families, friends, and communities.

Those of us instrumental in birthing Phoenix Community Church in Kalamazoo, Michigan, desired a worshiping community in which a rich diversity of rites of passage would be celebrated to mirror the lives of all the people—not just some. Members of Phoenix who are gay and lesbian felt a special urgency because too many crucial moments in our lives go unnoticed; too many life passages are entered and lived in isolation. We needed a spiritual home where we could tell our sacred stories, hear our exile literature read aloud, and celebrate the relationships and communities that have sustained us.

In fashioning rituals at Phoenix, we sometimes recovered symbols and images of the Christian tradition that we found to be still usable, and we sometimes created new ones. For the lesbian women at Phoenix particularly, it was vitally important to create new rituals that consciously break with patriarchal traditions. One tenet of patriarchal religion has been that the further one gets from one's body and one's sexual yearnings, the closer one comes to God. Lesbians, from our vantage points at the margins, know keenly how destructive such assumptions have been, and we are creating rituals that recognize the erotic as sacred power and celebrate the goodness of our sexual, sensual, embodied selves.

Carter Heyward is a lesbian, feminist priest and theologian who is keenly aware of how the Western Christian tradition has perpetuated a theology of dualisms between body and spirit, pleasure and virtue, sexuality and God. Heyward has devoted herself, in her priestly and teaching vocations, to healing these dualisms:

*I am attempting to give voice to an embodied—sensual—
relational movement among women and men who experience
our sexualities as a liberating resource and who, at least in
part through this experience, have been strengthened in the
struggle for justice for all. Patterns of sexual and gender injustice are linked inextricably to those of racial, economic, and
other structures of wrong relation. It follows that the liberation
of anyone depends on the tenacity of the connections and co-
alitions we are able to forge together. To do this work, we
must be able to envision these connections and embody this
tenacity.[6]*

One of the ways we envision the connections and embody the
tenacity to continue in the struggle for justice is by creating and
celebrating rituals that name the oppressive structures; that affirm
our capacity to invent new, more liberating and life-giving structures; and that keep alive our dreams of a world transformed.

Coming out is a life passage that is being recognized, honored,
and celebrated in ritual forms within lesbian and gay communities.
Coming out is akin to coming of age, but it doesn't necessarily
happen for lesbian and gay people during puberty. Coming-out
rituals are celebrations of rebirth, truth-telling, finding one's voice,
claiming the power to name, coming home to one's true identity,
and affirmation by a community that welcomes one home. Sometimes one takes a new name during a coming-out ritual, symboliz-
ing both the break with heterosexist definitions and the power to
name one's true identity.

At the celebration of a coming-out ritual, sometimes biological family members are present, sometimes not; for some of us,
coming out entails the loss of our biological families. However, for
many of us, coming-out rituals celebrate the development of new
connections in the present and the claiming of nonbiological ancestors as our mentors and guides. Such rituals are gatherings of the
"chosen families" that have loved and encouraged us into rebirth.

As noted earlier, lesbians and gay men are a minority without
minority biological families. We are, therefore, forced and freed to
understand family, kin, and community as being much broader than

the biological nuclear family. We are forced and freed to create new "family values" that move us beyond bloodlines. We are, in fact, fashioning new models of interdependence and community that might serve as an example to a wider society whose idolatrous worship of the nuclear family has fostered an ethic of "taking care of one's own."

Intriguing parallels exist between the original practice of baptism and contemporary coming-out rituals. In the early Christian church, baptism was a conscious decision by adults to publicly proclaim where they stood and with whom their lot was cast. In that sense, baptism was a coming-out ritual. Baptismal language and symbolism drew upon the Hebrew people's experience of a liberating exodus out of oppression, through the waters of the Red Sea. In a political context where identification with the Christian community was both dangerous and illegal, being baptized was risky: it signified a public declaration to work on behalf of justice and liberation for all peoples.

There are worshiping communities that make explicit reference to the parallels between baptismal and coming-out rituals. In a Christian context, coming-out rituals may incorporate symbols and language from baptismal renewal rites. For example, water may be poured on the head of the person whose coming out is being celebrated. The water recalls the birth waters of the womb, the waters of creation and rebirth, and the waters of the Red Sea. The ritual proclaims by word and symbol that this person has journeyed out of silence and death into new life and a new community. The creative interaction between ancient traditions and new ones is mutually enhancing. Not only are elements of baptismal rites incorporated into coming-out rituals, but the celebration of something as courageous and transforming as coming out recovers and illuminates the original meanings of baptism.

Increasingly, lesbian and gay couples are celebrating their commitment as life partners in covenant services. Our location on the margins frees us to fashion ritual elements that truly represent our lives rather than just mimic heterosexual marriage rites. We are deviants and outlaws who can proudly claim this location as we search for authentic words, acts, symbols, and music to celebrate this rite of passage. We are not constrained by traditions that force us into tight-fitting gowns, rigid seating arrangements, particular texts, or rules about who officiates. We can dress as we will, gather where we will, decorate the space with our own symbols, fashion our own covenant words, and invite those present to be full participants in the celebration.

In August of 1993, my partner, April, and I celebrated our decision to be lifelong companions in a covenant service. As we fashioned the service, we sought to maximize the participation of the friends and family members gathered with us. We had experienced too many heterosexual weddings as something akin to a spectator sport, where everyone sits, usually in rows, hushed and straining to see what is happening up front between the couple and the minister.

April and I put the altar in the middle of a circle of chairs. The two of us were seated for much of the service in that circle with others. When people arrived, they signed a covenant statement that now hangs on our wall. We all sang together at various times during the service. After April and I had spoken words of commitment to each other, our daughter Tanya joined us in a family covenant, and then all who were present were invited to say what this celebration meant to them. At the close of the service, family and friends spoke the following declaration to April and me:

> *In the presence of this good company*
> *In the presence of God*
> *By the power of your love*
> *By the power of the Spirit,*
> *Because you have exchanged vows of commitment,*
> *We recognize you as life partners.*[7]

Lesbians and gay men are fashioning new rituals for grieving the death of beloved partners and friends. The AIDS quilt, the largest folk art project in history, is a profoundly liturgical commemoration. Entering the field of quilt panels laid out near the Washington Monument was more impressive to me than entering the sanctuary of the cathedral of Notre Dame. As I walked among those panels, I felt a sense of awe and reverence that I have seldom experienced in church sanctuaries. And appropriately, in place of towering spires, the quilt focuses my gaze on the very earth which now enfolds the bodies of these sisters and brothers. Walking slowly from panel to panel, stopping to read, smile, and cry, was an experience of being on holy ground. I watched those who had found the panel of someone they knew, kneeling, tenderly touching the embroidered letters of their beloved friend's name and saying goodbye. The AIDS quilt, originating within gay communities and now also commemorating others who have died, is a powerful witness to the healing that can occur when death itself is brought out of the closet and is observed in a profoundly communal ritual that weaves together many cultures, races, and ages.

I am reminded of the death, a few years ago, of a man who sang in the local gay men's chorus. After the formal funeral service, in which neither this man's sexual orientation nor his commitment to the gay community was named, many of us felt the need for another service where the truth could be told and our friend could be remembered as he was. So, we gathered and told stories, prayed, laughed, cried, and held on to each other while the gay men's chorus sang the songs that our friend loved.

And finally, lesbians and gay men are fashioning celebrations that mark our life passages as a people. Such a celebration was held in New York City in the summer of 1994, when a parade brought out record numbers to commemorate the twenty-fifth anniversary of the Stonewall insurrection, a turning point in the emergence of the contemporary movement for lesbian and gay civil rights. And, oh, do we know how to throw a parade! Parades like the one in New York and the yearly Pride marches held throughout the nation are ritual celebrations of our communities' coming of age, coming out, and coming together in the struggle for justice.

The many and varied rituals being created to celebrate rites of passage in lesbian and gay communities are, indeed, tangible ways of envisioning connections and embodying tenacity in the struggle for justice. These ritual celebrations testify to the survival strength of lesbians and gay men who have persisted against enormous odds to love ourselves and one other and to keep community alive.

II

GRACE REVEALS

A NEW NAME

7

THE POWER OF SAYING
GOD-SHE

A friend, who I will call Carol, contacted me not long ago in great anguish. She told me that the careful contraceptive precautions that she and her husband, Paul, practiced had failed and she was pregnant. For a number of reasons, including age and physical complications in her last pregnancy, Carol could not imagine carrying, birthing, and raising another child.

Carol's religious upbringing had, however, ingrained in her the conviction that abortion was murder. Although she articulated many reasons to terminate the pregnancy, she feared that she and her husband might later regret an abortion. Her deepest fear, however, was that God would never forgive her.

After much turmoil, prayer, tears, conversation with friends, and vacillation, she and her husband chose to have the abortion. Carol and I talked often. I had no simple answers, but she didn't look to me for answers anyway. She needed me to hear her—her pain, her fear, and sense of desolation.

Because I live in another part of the country, I couldn't be with her physically the day she went for the abortion. I wanted, nevertheless, to be present with her somehow; so at the time I knew she was entering the clinic, I lit a candle and prayed for her. What transpired is difficult to describe.

At first, my prayers were beseeching, "Please, God, be with Carol, keep her safe. Please let her know she is loved, . . ." almost as though I needed to convince God that Carol deserved this divine attention. When I realized how I was praying, I chose consciously to address God as She, and my prayers changed. Instead of "please," I was saying, praying, "I know you know that sometimes we must face impossible, agonizing, tearing decisions. I know you know this pain and that you hold Carol tight at this moment, for she is your beloved."

Carol called me later that day and told me how Paul, against the policy of the doctor's office, had insisted on being present with her during the abortion. He had held her and wept with her. Carol expressed how, in Paul's touch and tears, she experienced God's presence. She said, "You know, before the surgery, I couldn't believe that God would be there or that He would ever forgive me. . . ." Carol paused. "He, She, whatever. . . ." She paused again and then said, "No, if God is a She, then God understands."

I then told Carol about my prayer experience that morning and my conviction that She does understand the struggle, the loss, and the pain. Carol replied, "Yes, I believe that now, too. I believe God was with me even there in that place I so dreaded to be."

This experience with Carol reaffirmed the power of language and images. It is impossible to exaggerate the impact that exclusively male language and imagery for God had on many of us as we were growing up. When the divine reality is spoken of and addressed only in male imagery such as "our heavenly Father," then girls and women never see themselves or their experiences mirrored in divine images. Rita Gross says:

> I am talking about the only thing we can talk about—images of God, not God. And I am talking about female images of God. Those images, it seems to me, should not be daring, degrading, or alien. If it is daring, degrading, or alienating to speak of God using female imagery and pronouns, that perhaps indicates something about the way women and the feminine are valued. Therefore, we might say that the ultimate symbol of our degradation is our inability to say "God-She."[1]

As women are speaking of God-She, we are discovering that there is more at stake than a change of pronouns. There is no less at stake than a radical change in the way of seeing the world, ourselves, human relationships, and the divine reality. Patriarchal theology not only viewed men and women as opposites in an up-down power relationship but heaven was divorced from earth, God was seen as above creation rather than in the midst of it, and the spirit or soul was seen as separate from the material or bodily. Patriarchal theology taught that the further one gets from one's body, the earth, and one's sexuality, the closer one comes to God.

Feminist and womanist theologies are seeking to heal the split between body and spirit, earth and heaven, love and justice, personal faith and active concern for the world.

In my work with Leaven, I have been privileged to lead seminars for women titled *In Our Own Voice: Women Reshaping Theology and Spirituality*. In these seminars, we explore images for God—old images that are no longer meaningful to us—and new ways to give expression to what we experience as holy. It is remarkable what emerges out of the shared silence as we express these images in poems, sculptures, drawings, and paintings. On one retreat, we came up with more than fifty words that describe the holy for us—names for God; words such as:

> *breath*
> *breath within our breath*
> *holy sound*
> *water of all life*
> *fire*
> *lover*
> *sea sharp wash of truth*
> *pouring forth love*
> *unavoidable one*
> *dependably present mystery*
> *a friend is God with skin on*
> *comforter*
> *challenger . . . nudge*
> *shelterer*
> *quiet sustenance*
> *passionate joy*

Such an exercise reminds us that the divine mystery has many names. No one name or even many names can capture or definitively name the One who is always surprising us by bursting the boundaries of human language and human custom. The power of saying God-She recalls to us the original grace of our createdness in God's image.

> *In the beginning, long before there was any idea of God, something stirred. In that cosmic moment pulsating in possibility, God breathed into space and, groaning in passion and pain and hope, gave birth to creation. . . . It was far better than we can imagine. For coming forth from God/in God/with God/by God, we were shaped by God, in God's own image, formed in the being of God, daughters and sons of God. With all created beings, we are reflections of/witnesses to God's own possibility. It was very, very good.*[2]

8

GOOD SHAME / BAD SHAME

For from the least to the greatest of them,
everyone is greedy for unjust gain;
and from prophet to priest,
everyone deals falsely.
They have treated the wound of
my people carelessly,
saying, "Peace, peace,"
when there is no peace.
They acted shamefully . . .
yet they were not ashamed,
they did not know how to blush.
          —JEREMIAH 6:13–15A

From a very early age, I felt at home in overalls and jeans and experienced distress whenever I wore a dress. Unlike my sisters, I was not particularly attracted to dolls or tea parties or other indoor games. Every chance I got, I would be outdoors, fantasizing that my bicycle was a powerful motorcycle or that I was winning a marathon bicycle race. I was playing every sport imaginable—baseball, football, basketball, ice hockey, tennis. It also happened that when we moved from Chicago to East Lansing, Michigan, we came to live on a block where most of the children my age were boys.

Throughout grade school, I played sports in school and in the neighborhood. I was captain of the Marble Elementary School football team—the only girl on an all-male team. There were some good things about this cross-gender behavior: I felt pride in being different from the other girls; up to a certain age, the boys were admiring of my athletic skills; my parents were supportive of my unorthodox dress and activities. However, I also experienced moments of shame at being different.

When I was seven, we had a babysitter named Karen. She had long blond hair, was thin and well proportioned, wore makeup and perfume, and had amazing fingernails that she painted a different color every time she came to sit for us. I was in awe of her femininity. I also thought she was strikingly beautiful.

Just prior to my eighth birthday, I was telling Karen what we'd planned for my party. She asked me how many kids were invited. I started adding them up on my fingers, "Let's see, Larry and Roger, David, Jimmy and Carl, Stan, Bill Long, and Billy Rogers. Eight!" I announced proudly.

"Yes," she said, "and who else?"

I looked at her with puzzlement and proceeded to count off again, "Roger, Billy, Carl. . . . That's it!"

"Are you sure that there aren't any other children coming?" she asked.

I didn't get it. I thought maybe she knew of someone I was forgetting. But how would she know my friends? I shook my head "no," there were no other children coming.

"Are there no girls?" she asked. "Only boys?" Her tone was one of utter disbelief.

"Those are my friends," I protested, never realizing before that moment that I had no girlfriends.

Karen threw back her long neck and hair and laughed in a way I had never heard her laugh before. She was laughing at me—or so I thought. I became flushed, felt exposed, humiliated. I wanted to run away. And then rage sprung up in me. I suddenly hated her for making me feel so small, so odd, and so deficient.

It was a shame experience. To feel shame, explains psychologist Gershen Kaufman, "is to feel *seen* in a painfully diminished sense. The self feels exposed both to itself and to anyone else present. . . . Contained in the experience of shame is the piercing awareness of ourselves as fundamentally deficient in some vital way as a human being."[1]

Shame involves a sense of feeling naked and intensely self-conscious in a tormenting way that has a paralyzing effect.[2] It can result in a vicious cycle: we find it difficult to talk directly about the experience because it feels too shameful, leaving us even more isolated and alone.[3]

As in my experience with Karen, shame often results from a person of significance breaking what Kaufman calls the interpersonal bridge that is so necessary in relationships. Trust seems suddenly, unexpectedly betrayed as the trusted person becomes someone who judges, rejects, blames, finds fault with, or belittles us.[4]

Much shame is unintentionally induced. I doubt that Karen wanted to shame me. Some shame is, however, intended: for example, when parents say things like, "Shame on you. How could you do such a thing? How could you embarrass me that way? You ought to be ashamed of yourself."

Shame also gets recycled and passed on from generation to generation as children perceive—from either words or actions—that certain things cause their parents shame, and the children mimic their parents' shame.

I've discovered in recent years that I have considerable shame about being tired. I ought to be able to do everything I set out to do in a day—no matter how long the list—without feeling worn out or on the point of exhaustion. The disabling effect of the shame, of course, is that I've developed defense mechanisms against it which cut me off from actually allowing myself to acknowledge, feel, and attend to my fatigue. This means I only get more worn out.

Rationally, I know that there's nothing wrong with a body being tired, but emotionally it's another matter. I feel I'm somehow deficient if I'm tired. By observing my parents in recent years, I've learned where this shame comes from. Although they didn't directly communicate it to me, they both have difficulty acknowledging and accepting their own fatigue.

One of the areas of life that most of us have received shamed-based messages about is sexuality. We see this experience in a two-year-old who comes to Mother with a dirty diaper for the third time that day and meets with frowns, anger, and disapproval; in the child who is caught masturbating and receives the message—verbally or nonverbally—that such behavior is shameful; in the ten-year-old who has to admit to wetting the bed one more time; in the teenaged girl who feels that menstruation is somehow shameful and hides the box of sanitary pads on the top shelf of the closet or feels conspicuous holding it in the store's checkout line.

From early childhood on, we develop strategies of defense against shame. There are external defenses and internal defenses. Kaufman has identified the external defense strategies as: blaming, rage, contempt, striving for power, striving for perfection, and internal withdrawal.[5] If I feel shame, I may try to defend against it by blaming someone else for the offense that is so unacceptable to me.

Recently, a friend of mine lent her car to her brother. He parked it in his driveway and let his two-year-old son, Matthew, play in it while he was working in the backyard. The little boy somehow dislodged the brake, and the car rolled down the driveway and hit a tree. Although Matthew was uninjured, his father—unable to bear the shame he apparently felt—blamed first his wife, for not watching the little boy, and then my friend, for lending him the car. When he returned the keys, he exclaimed, in Matthew's presence, "Matthew nearly totaled your car!" By assigning the blame to his two-year-old son, he only deepened Matthew's shame.

Each of us has different defenses against shame. In some cases we learn to disown our feelings, needs, and drives.[6] If we learn, for example, in our families of origin that crying when we feel hurt or sad is "being a baby," we will learn to feel shame when tears well up. If we never see either parent cry, we will most likely intuit that our parents are rejecting and perhaps contemptuous of the expression of sadness or hurt.

When a terrified little girl repeatedly fails to be seen, recognized, held, and comforted in her fear, she learns to reject that little girl herself. Later in life, as a defense against her shame, she may not even recognize when she is afraid. And she is also likely to become rejecting of others who express their fear.

The more deeply we internalize shame, the more profoundly

we reject certain parts of ourselves as shameful, even splitting them off. Through this internalization of shame, we thereby take up the task of shaming ourselves.

The shame that I have been talking about thus far is what I would call "bad shame." I don't want to heap shame upon shame by calling it "bad." I simply want to say, thereby, that it is harmful shame, shame that limits our growth and our capacity to feel deeply and become fully human. There is nothing wrong with the various defense strategies that I have named. They are *all* necessary; we *had* to develop them to survive. But they become counterproductive and harmful when they become rigid and automatic, when we have no choice about them, when they cut us off from people who are not a threat to us. That kind of shame, and the defenses we have developed to hide from feeling it, is shame that requires healing.

There is another kind of shame: "good" shame. Good shame is not a barrier but an avenue to growth, deeper compassion, and fuller humanity. It is appropriate to experience a degree of shame when we violate an internally prized value, when we harm or violate another person, or when we break a trust or a commitment. In such instances, we may feel shame for breaking the interpersonal bridge. Good shame, as I am speaking of it, is not a weapon to diminish ourselves but rather the recognition that our deeds, words, gestures have harmed another. At such moments, we may feel disappointed in ourselves, but I would never argue that we should therefore punish ourselves relentlessly. Admitting our humanness, acknowledging the failing, we may blush and feel some anger with ourselves, but we should not allow ourselves to enter the vicious cycle of shame, wanting to disappear or beat ourselves into nonbeing.

There is another kind of shame that I would call "good" or "functional" in this time when so much is called "dysfunctional." It is the shame that the prophet Jeremiah said was singularly missing among the leaders of his day: "they did not know how to blush," he said. None of them seemed to know the difference between injustice and justice, between truth and falsehood. They committed injustice; they committed violence and called it peace; and they did not feel shame. They did not blush.

There ought to be some blushing going on today as we learn

that the wealthiest 10 percent of our country's people increased their wealth in the 1980s by 128 percent while those who comprise the poorest 10 percent became 10 percent poorer during the same years. I think there ought to be some blushing and some appropriate shame expressed.

Shame, pain, and anger are closely connected emotions that surface when those of us who are white begin to wake up and shake off some of the numbing lies we have been fed in a racist society. In those first stages of waking up, we discover how much we didn't know, didn't see, and didn't feel. The systemic nature of racism effectively anesthetizes white people against feeling the pain of racism. We do not feel our own pain and we are shielded from hearing the pain of people of color. As Robert Terry has observed: "To be white in America is not to have to think about it."[7]

Joseph Barndt, a white anti-racist activist, describes his first awareness of this anesthetized state. He was participating in an inter-racial seminar when an African American woman expressed her impatience with the frequent intellectualizing by white participants:

> You people really don't give a damn! But it's not that you
> don't want to. You just don't know how to. You don't know
> how to feel! Your heads have been cut off from your guts, and
> you've lost touch with your own feelings. . . . You have been
> anesthetized to the agony of the destruction inside yourselves.
> If you could see and feel the effects of racism on your own
> people, you would not be able to tolerate it. You would not
> be able to control your anger . . . But you white people have
> lost your ability to feel . . .[8]

A sense of shame may be the first sign that we are waking up and beginning to face the enormity of the crimes committed by our white ancestors in the past and the devastation that racism wreaks in the present. As the poet Julia de Burgos writes: "That my grandfather was a slave is my grief; had he been a master that would have been my shame."[9]

Shame followed denial and disbelief when I first began to study the true history of how European Americans deceived, betrayed, and massacred Native Americans. Racism has effectively protected white people from having to learn about their own history. It would scarcely occur to this nation's leaders to build a holocaust museum that would offer tangible reminders of how,

> *from 1607 to the Wounded Knee massacre in 1890, approximately one-fourth of all tribes permanently disappeared, and the Native American population decreased from an estimated 2 to 5 million to 200,000, an attrition rate unmatched by the Black Plague, the Thirty Years' War, or any modern war.[10]*

Shame may be a first reaction to the pervasiveness of institutionalized racism, but shame needs to give way to something deeper if white people are serious about challenging racism. Without a commitment to confronting racism in ourselves and in the places where we live, work, and worship, we become mired in defensiveness and self-pity. Racism needs to be eliminated not because white people need to be relieved of shame, but because "white individuals and white communities . . . benefit from precisely those structures that undermine and destroy individuals and communities of color."[11]

White people often seek forgiveness from people of color to lessen the shame they feel. The shame I am calling "appropriate" or "good" is, in the context of white racism, not healed by simply appealing for forgiveness. It is healed by a commitment to the work of anti-racism. Nancy Richardson believes that unless white people can move beyond "a vague sense of dis-ease," they will continue to exhibit symptoms that "run the gamut from denial to guilt, from arrogance to self-pity, from defensiveness to passivity."

> *Without tools for accurate diagnosis of the disease, appropriate steps toward health are impossible. In order to develop these tools, it is essential that we as white people learn to understand the history of this country and our place in it, that we recognize ways in which we collaborate with white supremacist policies and practices, that we develop communities of resistance, and that we participate in collaborative strategies for transformation. In order to do this, we need to be honest with*

each other, to avoid self-righteousness, to provide mutual self-criticism without succumbing to self-pity or guilt-tripping, and to receive challenge from colleagues as evidence of support.[12]

One further illustration of the difference between good and bad shame, or appropriate and inappropriate shame, is the response that we had, as citizens of the United States, to the Vietnam War. As we were disengaging from that war, we had an opportunity to acknowledge and express appropriate shame; to talk honestly about the reasons we had entered the conflict. We could have learned from the war. Instead, we covered that shame with a different kind of shame: we found it shameful to have lost or failed; we felt humiliated by a tiny, "underdeveloped" country. Our sense of shame and self-contempt unfortunately was turned against the returning veterans who were rendered invisible or openly rejected, not because we disagreed with what they did but because they were living symbols of our defeat and humiliation.

Although we hear people say that the Vietnam War was "wrong," they often phrase their analyses of what was wrong about the war in such statements as "We should never have gotten involved in something we couldn't win." That the war was "wrong" in a moral sense has seldom been discussed openly in the political arena. We might have owned appropriate shame about this war, shame that could have contributed to our growth and maturity as a nation. Instead, Vietnam became a symbol of humiliation and defeat that was not discussed openly for nearly two decades—except in Rambo movies, which glorified fantasized acts of revenge to reverse the humiliation. Without appropriate shame, we needed a victory to undo our sense of defeat. During the Gulf War, then President George Bush triumphantly declared that we had finally put the Vietnam "syndrome" behind us.

Unfortunately, there are no magic formulas for emerging from debilitating, "inappropriate" shame—the kind of shame that spirals into self-contempt. We can, however, experience moments of grace-filled intimacy that help us move through a time of shame. When I am tired, for example, it can be immensely important for friends to let me not only be tired but also express my shame.

Friends offer me shelter and nurture when that tired, scared, ashamed little girl appears in all her vulnerability. April holds me and lets me know that I am loved as I am, tired or strong, weak or full of vitality. I have even allowed myself, in the past couple of years, the luxury of imaging God as tender, sheltering arms that allow me to lean into them as I am—tired, ashamed, and all.

When I can lean into that divine presence or the welcoming love of friends, I let go of shame that would discount my weariness. And I am able to hear again, "You are my beloved with whom I am well pleased."

9

HUMILITY RECONSIDERED

[God] has told you, O mortal, what
is good;
and what does [God] require of you
but to do justice, and to love
kindness,
and to walk humbly with your God.
                                        —MICAH 6:8

According to the prophet Micah, being fully alive and in deepest relationship with God consists of three things: doing justice, loving kindness, and walking humbly with God. We can probably identify with doing justice and loving kindness, but walking humbly with God? There's that word, "humility"! Walking humbly with God conjures up images of being led, keeping quiet, and exhibiting subservience.

Can this be what the prophet Micah was talking about when he spoke of walking humbly with God? He has just declared that God doesn't really care about many of the things that we call "religious"; that what God yearns for is that we live with integrity—with compassion and an abiding sense of justice. Rather than subservience or submission, the synonyms for "humility" are words like "reverence" and "gratitude." Reverence and gratitude acknowledge life as a precious gift. Humility is the recognition that none of us—not even God—exists outside of relatedness. We are all part of one another.

Alice Walker, in her novel *The Color Purple*, gives us a beautiful description of humility, spoken by Shug in her conversation with Celie:

Listen, God love everything you love—and a mess of stuff you don't. But more than anything else, God love admiration.
You saying God vain? I ast.
Naw, she say. Not vain, just wanting to share a good thing. I think it pisses God off if you walk by the color purple in a field somewhere and don't notice it.
What it do when it pissed off? I ast.
Oh, it make something else. People think pleasing God is all God care about. But any fool living in the world can see it always trying to please us back.
Yeah? I say.
Yeah, she say. It always making little surprises and springing them on us when us least expect.[1]

Being humble doesn't mean groveling or making oneself small. Humility is a liberating, empowering sense that this life, this earth, the air we breathe, other humans, and all living creatures are precious gifts to be reverenced. Humility has gotten such a bad name precisely because it has been taken from this context of relationship and connectedness and put in a context of up/down power and dominance. Many of us have learned that humility is a spiritual virtue quite the opposite of arrogance and boastfulness. So we think that to be humble means to be modest, self-effacing, and not overly impressed with oneself, and certainly not to blow one's own horn. Being humble means that when you get a compliment, you should say, "Oh, it was nothing really."

Someone years ago showed me a different meaning of humility. In grade school, I had a friend named Sarah. We walked home from school together, and we would often stop to visit Sarah's Aunt Irma. She would meet us at the door beaming and usher us into the kitchen where cookies or cake fresh from the oven waited for us.

Aunt Irma sat at the table with us, listening intently to our stories, frowning and sympathizing when we reported some terrible injustice at the hands of a teacher and laughing at our silly jokes. She wasn't overbearing or intrusive. When she sensed we wanted to be left alone, she did that, and I remember her moving through the rooms singing to herself.

Aunt Irma had a peculiar trait that completely intrigued Sarah and me. When we complimented her on her delicious cookies, she didn't say, "Oh, they're nothing special." Nor did she say, "This batch isn't quite right; I should've added more butter." She didn't even say, "thank you." Instead, she reached for a cookie, tasted it, nodded, and said, "You know, you're right, these cookies are great!"

This happened not just with cookies but with most everything we complimented her about—her hair, her clothes, her house, her knitting. If one of us said, "I like your blouse, Aunt Irma," she'd get up from the table, go to the mirror in the hallway, turn around, and look at the blouse from different angles, exclaiming, "It does look nice, doesn't it!"

This struck Sarah and me as funny. We'd both been taught that when you receive a compliment, you're obligated to say "thank you" at the very least, and sometimes humility dictated that you add, "This blouse? Oh, it's just an old blouse I've had for a long time." So, it became a game for Sarah and me to try and get Aunt Irma, just one time, to say "thank you" to one of our compliments. But every time we complimented her, she joined in with something like "Why yes, you're right, it *is* beautiful, it *is* delicious!" And Sarah and I would peek at each other and stifle giggles.

Some people might observe Aunt Irma's behavior and say she lacked humility, but I believe she exhibited humility. Because, when we—in our mischievous way—pointed to something she wore or made, she sat up and took notice. She looked at the object with us, as though seeing it for the first time, and she expressed delight and enjoyment. When she tasted a cookie, looked in the mirror, or studied the pattern in her knitting, her delight and enjoyment revealed that these things were gifts for her also—gifts she could reverence with us. She was saying, time and again, "Yes, yes, isn't it wonderful?! Aren't there wonderful things to be seen and heard and tasted and touched and done?"

Aunt Irma expressed robust delight in common, ordinary

things. She wasn't afraid to claim her part in bringing these things into being, nor was she focused inordinately on herself. She helped me to see that there are gifts everywhere to delight in. Like Shug, she was saying, "God love everything you love, and a mess of stuff you don't. People think pleasing God is all God care about. But any fool living in the world can see God always trying to please us back. God always making little surprises and springing them on us when we least expect." Aunt Irma was fully alive to the gifts and surprises on every hand and she had the capacity to express uninhibited, robust delight. Expressing that delight is, I believe, something of what it means to walk humbly with God.

10

The Cross and the Triangle

I always wear two symbols that say something about my identity, my people, my faith, and my commitments: a triangle around my neck and a cross on a ring. Only recently have I come to realize how interrelated these two symbols are. Both represent a means whereby people were put to death. Both have become symbols of movements that say "no" to death and "yes" to life.

The cross was a form of execution Roman authorities used in the days when Palestine was forcibly annexed into the Roman Empire. Criminals convicted of such things as murder, theft, and crimes against the state were nailed to the cross and left to die, slowly and torturously.

The black and pink triangles had their origins in the concentration camps of Germany under the Third Reich. The followers of Adolf Hitler scapegoated a number of different groups and marked them for extermination. Jewish people were the main targets. Prostitutes, communists, gypsies, people with mental illness or developmental and physical disabilities, and gay and lesbian people were among other groups considered threats to the Aryan race.

In the death camps, one of the many indignities prisoners underwent was to be forced to sew a badge onto their striped prison uniforms. Jews had to sew a yellow Star of David onto their uniforms. Prostitutes and lesbians had to wear black triangles; communists, red triangles; and gay men, pink triangles.

Pink and black triangles have become symbols of the contemporary lesbian/gay civil rights movement, symbols of pride, resistance, and solidarity. But to understand the full meaning of the symbols, it is essential to remember the origins of the black and pink triangles. Wearing one of these triangles is a way of remembering the suffering of thousands of sisters and brothers. To wear it is to say, "Never again. We will not be silent. The way to honor the dead is to work for justice now." The triangle shape should also remind us that homophobia and anti-Semitism often go hand in hand.

It is risky to wear the pink or black triangle. In Germany, it singled you out for death. During World War II, King Christian X of Denmark (who was not Jewish) wore the Star of David as an act of solidarity and resistance. Too few people joined him. Today, wearing the triangles may cause you to risk losing your job, associates, and church membership; it may also make you subject to harassment and violence. Occasionally, heterosexual friends and advocates dare to wear the pink triangle, but most people do not, for fear of guilt by association.

It used to be a risky and politically dangerous thing to wear a cross. The early followers of Jesus were part of an underground movement. If they were publicly identified with their executed leader, they faced imprisonment, torture, and sometimes death. A minister once underscored this point by taking down the sanctuary cross on Good Friday and putting in its place a replica of an electric chair. He then turned to the parishioners and asked how many of them would want to wear a little replica of an electric chair on a chain around their necks.

Jesus' physical life ended on a cross because the kind of life he lived was a threat to the dominant powers. Jesus tried to warn people that joining his movement would be costly and politically dangerous. When he spoke of "taking up your cross and following me," he was warning his disciples that they too could be arrested, brought before the authorities, and executed.

From the early beginnings of Christianity through the centuries to this day, there have been Christians who have understood the cross as a sign of warning, resistance, and hope. Unfortunately, a different understanding of the cross gained ascendancy as the Jesus story was depoliticized, taken out of its historical context, and robbed of its social vision. Individual salvation and heaven became the goals of believers rather than living now as though God's reign were present on earth as it is in heaven. This theology also asserted that it was God's plan for Jesus to die on the cross in order to cleanse us of our sins.

There are Jews who choose not to use the word "holocaust" when referring to the German death camps; they speak rather of "*Shoah,*" the Hebrew word for annihilation. Prior to its application in the Nazi context, "holocaust" had sometimes referred to a sacrificial offering to God, which implies a redemptive purpose. Therefore, some people understandably do not want to imply by using the word "holocaust" that the Nazi attempt to destroy the Jews and other peoples had any redemptive purpose.

Something similar occurs in relation to the cross. To say that God is present with those who suffer is very different from saying that God wills suffering. To say that God's Spirit can be called upon to sustain us in times of trial and persecution is very different from saying that God desires for us to enter times of trial and persecution. Jesus remained faithful to his vision of love, even forgiving his enemies as he was breathing his last on the cross. That is very different from saying that God wanted Jesus to die on the cross.

The cross represents a way of living with radical love, resistance to oppression, and reverence for life. For the disciples of Jesus to wear a cross then was something like wearing a black or pink triangle today. It was a statement of hope and the conviction that death can be transformed.

The triangle has spiritual significance for me because it recalls suffering but does not glorify it. By choosing to remember the suffering of those who died in the death camps, we express our conviction that their suffering can be transformed by our solidarity and by our resistance to death in all its forms. The triangle has spiritual significance because God is present wherever human beings suffer and is known most intimately by people who have experienced oppression.

I wear the triangle not only as a way of coming out as a lesbian but as a way of saying that I will remember the suffering it symbolizes by working for justice today. In a similar fashion, I wear a cross not only as a way of coming out as a Christian but as a way of saying that I will not forget the passionate and compassionate way that Jesus lived and died. I will remember his suffering by working to alleviate suffering wherever I can.

I wear a triangle and a cross because both say something about who my people are. I wear a triangle to identify with my lesbian sisters and gay brothers. I wear a cross to identify with a liberation movement and subculture within Christianity that are alive around the world.

I wear the triangle as a symbol both of warning and hope: warning that terrible crimes have been and can be perpetrated against lesbians and gay men; hope that a new and different day will come. I wear the cross in remembrance of Jesus' words of warning and hope: warning that the life of faith is costly; hope that even though the body may be killed, the dream cannot—as long as we act with passion and boldness to keep it alive.

11

IN THIS *KAIROS* MOMENT

The incident has haunted me since hearing of it several years ago. Marienella García served as director of the Human Rights Commission in El Salvador and for years risked imprisonment and death by publicly exposing human rights violations and working with the poor for land reform. In March 1983, she was found dead after having been abducted and tortured. The government forbade a public memorial service in the church where her body lay. Soldiers were dispatched to guard the church entrance and ensure that only the priest would be present at the Mass and funeral.

Fearing the consequences of disobeying the government's decree, most people stayed away. But some of the poorest peasants with whom Marienella had worked went to the church that day and walked right past the guards into the sanctuary. One by one, with the soldiers looking on, they knelt by the open casket in prayer, kissed their beloved friend and advocate, and said their goodbyes. Later that night, under the cover of darkness, the army raided the homes of these mourners, arresting the men and raping the women.

Before hearing that story, I had never fully realized the great peril at which another group of women went to the grave of their beloved friend and advocate on the first Easter morning. It was the grave of a convicted, crucified, political criminal, over which guards stood watch, ready to report the identities of any who dared to show support. The tardiness of my realization is strange, considering that Scripture describes the rest of the disciples as hiding, lying low, avoiding guilt by association and its consequent punishment.

The courage of these women on that morning is the first sign of a resurrection faith. By going to the grave, Mary, Joanna, and Mary Magdalene declared that they would not forget who he was and what he stood for. This act of remembering was a far riskier choice than we may at first assume.

A remarkable encounter then occurred at the grave. The women at first were perplexed to find an empty grave, but then they heard, "Why do you seek the living among the dead?" At first, this sounds like a reprimand: "Why have you come here? This isn't where you are supposed to be!" But it was not a reprimand. For these women—who dared to come and stand at the place of danger, loss, and abandonment—perceived that resurrection was not only about their beloved teacher, Jesus; it was also a *kairos* moment in their own lives. They were brought to choosing life with the knowledge that the same power their teacher had lived from was available to them. Even in the face of official violence, the intimidation of the soldiers, and the cynical voices of those who said that things could never change, these women realized that resurrection means living from God's dream for creation. Being faithful to that dream means keeping it alive by responding to ever new *kairos* moments, when traditions shatter like a rock that cracks as seeds of new life push through and shoots appear from the earth, bringing forth new buds. The women remember that God is a God of the living: "From this time forward I make you hear new things, hidden things that you have not known. They are created now, not long ago; before today you have never heard of them, so that you could not say: 'I already knew them.' . . . I am about to do a new thing; now it springs forth, do you not perceive it?" (Isa. 48:6–7; 43:19).

So, the women left the grave and told the rest of the disciples what they had experienced. They were alive with the good news that not death, nor fear, nor tradition, nor intimidation can kill the dream of God's shalom, where justice and peace shall embrace. They came to tell the other disciples that what seems like a dead end is actually a beginning. However, the others met their testimony and spiritual experience with disbelief, discounting it as nothing more than "an idle tale."

It is not coincidental that women were the first to understand the *kairos* challenge of that Easter morning; it is not coincidental that the poorest of the poor were faithful witnesses to the meaning of Marienella García's life and death. Nor is it coincidental that it is the voices of the poor and oppressed around the world who are calling us to respond to the *kairos* of our times. For they know what the people of Israel, who were in slavery, knew—that God is not indifferent to the pain of the oppressed. God is not impartial; God chooses, then and now, the side of the victims and empowers them to claim their liberation.

It is also not coincidental that the testimony of the women on that first Easter morning was thought to be only an idle tale. For women's words often have been discounted as gossip in an attempt to silence their voices, and women's vision often has been belittled as inconsequential.

In some seminaries today, feminist theologians are sometimes dismissed as overly emotional or strident and told that they are not doing "real" theology because they obviously have an ideological "ax to grind." Women in our churches who give voice to their pain about the exclusively male language and images for God that permeate our hymns, our prayers, our scripture readings, and our sermons are often dismissed with irritation at their insistence that a change of pronouns should matter so much. "Aren't there more important matters that we should be attending to?" some people ask. "Besides, the male pronouns and images are not meant to exclude . . . why can't these women understand that?"

Indeed, there is more at stake than a change of pronouns. Women and men with a feminist consciousness would have us hear that no less is at stake than a radical change in the way we see the world, God, ourselves, and human relationships. This is a *kairos* moment. The foundations have been shaken; new patterns of relating between women and men are emerging; old assumptions about gender differences are being challenged; economic and political inequities between women and men are being exposed and confronted; new images of God are being explored; and old, eclipsed images are being resurrected.

It is a frightening time, as all *kairos* times are, for the ground on which we walked seems to sway and buckle under our feet. It is also a time of promise, as all *kairos* times are, for it may be that, here and now, God is doing a new thing; this moment it may come to fruition. Can we perceive it? Can we listen to the voices of women and men who are holding before us a feminist vision? What are they saying to us about this *kairos* time?

First of all, they are saying that if we are to understand the *kairos* of our own times in terms of gender, we must understand the historical roots of sexism and patriarchy in our Jewish and Christian heritage. Similarly, we must search to rediscover those historical and biblical roots that go against the grain of sexism.

The word "patriarchy" is derived from the Latin and Greek words for "father" (*pater*). A patriarch was the paternal leader of a tribe or family. Although patriarchy did not originate with the Jewish and Christian traditions, its legacy is amply evident in both testaments.

> *Patriarchy has been described as a way of structuring reality in terms of good / evil, redemption / guilt, authority / obedience, reward / punishment, power / powerless, haves / have-nots, master / slave. The first in each opposite was assigned to the patriarchal father, or the patriarch's Father God, frequently indistinguishable from one another, the second to women as "the other" and in time to all "others" who could be exploited. The father did the naming, the owning, the controlling, the ordering, the forgiving, the giving, considering himself capable of making the best decisions for all.[1]*

The patriarchy of the Bible was made vividly clear to me when my mother and I were asked to lead a mother and daughter retreat for a church women's group. The group specifically requested that we do some Bible study about mother-daughter relationships. In searching the pages of the Hebrew and Christian scriptures for a story about a mother and a daughter, we could find only one! Mark's Gospel describes the tenacious faith of the Syrophoenician woman who implores Jesus to heal her daughter (Mark 7:24–30). Even though this mother-daughter story is inspiring, my mother and I were stunned to discover that this was the only story in which the divine presence is imaged in a mother-daughter relationship. There are all kinds of parent-child stories in the Bible; some involve fathers, some involve mothers, but always the child is male. We are all familiar with the stories of Abraham and Isaac, David and Absalom, and the parable of the prodigal son. Sarah, Hannah, Elizabeth, and Mary are all waiting for the birth of a baby boy.

Patriarchy has oppressed women, but it also has exacted a price from men, forcing them to live up to certain ideals of manhood and masculinity. As Nelle Morton points out, "patriarchy polarized human beings by gender and endowed each gender with certain roles and properties so that neither could experience full humanness."[2] Patriarchal spirituality has tended to go hand in hand with a dualistic, hierarchical vision of the world. God is good, humans are sinners; the soul partakes of the divine, the flesh partakes of that which decays.

Some early Church "Fathers" taught that the human body is a burden to the spiritual life rather than a source of inspiration or a medium for celebration. Those who would be spiritual, they argued, must strive to master the body. Women, they said, are the "weaker sex" because they are closer to the earth, the body, and the base emotions, more given to deceit and fickleness. Men are more "innately" suited for spiritual and intellectual pursuits; they are identified with rationality, order, authority, and power. Women are identified with irrationality, chaos, superstition, and sensuality.

Through the centuries, from biblical times to our own, some voices have challenged these assumptions. Women and men in our day are calling us to reimage God and faith in ways that are consonant with a counterstream within the scriptures that challenges patriarchy. Allow me, in the next few paragraphs, to sketch a few elements that characterize feminist theology and spirituality.

Women are finding power, energy, and authority in metaphors and images that do not identify God with the high and mighty but with those of low estate, as Mary said in her Magnificat. Women's own experience of marginalization has sparked a sensitivity to suffering and pain wherever it occurs. Feminist theology grows directly out of the pain of invisibility, voicelessness, and oppression, and it joins hands with other liberation theologies around the world in celebrating a hope, a joyous unity, and a sense of divine presence that others find mysterious in circumstances that would seem to engender despair.

Where women are engaged in psychology, theology, the arts, and music, common metaphors are emerging to express the nature of human beings and of God—metaphors of connection, of relation, of tapestry and weaving, of circles and expanding spirals, of wholeness and mutuality.

It is no accident that storytelling has been a primary means of women's theologizing: experience is valued as a primary source of spiritual wisdom, and authority is inherent in the integrity of experience. As Mary Pellauer has stated, "If there is anything worth calling theology, it is listening to people's stories—listening to them and honoring and cherishing them, and asking them to become even more brightly beautiful than they already are."[3]

Increasingly, women are finding that differences in race, abilities, gender, age, culture, and sexual orientation are not to be feared or erased: such differences provide us with new insights and richness as well as an enlargement of our own individual perspective.

Sexuality, rather than being the source of sin in the world, can be celebrated as a gift of the Creator. Although sexuality can be abused, the sin arises from dominance and exploitation, not from sexuality in and of itself. The division between body and spirit is being healed by women as they trust the body's wisdom, dance and circle, touch, and accept themselves as incarnations of Spirit.

A feminist vision also argues that the spiritual life cannot be divorced from an active concern for the world. Love and justice are inseparable realities. In contrast to a view of the self and faith that is rational, disembodied, and individualistic, a feminist vision of self and faith argues that we are embodied, passionate, and relational beings.

Finally, a feminist vision realizes that language is not "mere" semantics but the means by which our very selfhood and the selfhood of God are either expressed or bypassed. In chapter 7 we noted Rita Gross's observation that to hold the opinion that it is degrading or alienating to address God as "She" reveals how one values women. "The ultimate symbol of our degradation," says Gross, "is our inability to say 'God-She.'"[4]

The truth of Gross's remark was brought home to me when I was asked to preach in a small-town church which had chosen to focus that Sunday on the gifts and ministry of women. The liturgist for the service was a member of the congregation, whom I will call Carol. Carol lives on a farm, and for the children's time she had brought some photographs that showed the birth of a baby lamb. Only the mother sheep was in the pictures with the little lamb—the male of the species was not around at that point. Carol engaged the children by asking them what the mother sheep did for her baby. "She licks it," the children answered. "She gives it milk. . . ." "Yes," said Carol, "the mother loves the little lamb, doesn't she? She protects her baby and tenderly cares for it. The baby lamb is very, very precious to her."

And then Carol asked, "And who does that mother sheep remind you of?" The children shrugged their shoulders, and then one little girl exclaimed that her cat had some kittens and she licked them. "Yes," said Carol, "but does the love of this mother sheep remind you of someone else?"

I was incredulous. I thought: She is going to do it! How wonderful! She is going to say, "The love of this mother sheep is like the love of God, because God loves each and every one of us." But then Carol answered her own question with these words, "Doesn't it remind you of your mothers and how they love you? Your mothers protect you and care for you. So, this week try and remember how your mothers love you and that you could maybe say, 'Thanks, Mom' sometime this week."

It apparently had not occurred to Carol to see the love of this mother sheep (or the love of the children's mothers) as an image of God's love. Very likely neither Carol nor anyone else in that church had ever heard the divine imaged in female terms. Immediately after that children's time, we prayed together, children and adults: "Our *Father*, who art in heaven. . . ." And I thought: What does it mean for these people—especially for the girls and women in this congregation—to have never seen or heard themselves mirrored in divine images?

One of the things that inclusive language does for all of us is remind us that *all* of our language about God is metaphorical. When we say with the psalmist, "God is the *rock* of my salvation," we understand that God's faithfulness is steadfast *like* a rock. But when we only speak of "Father" and never of "Mother" when referring to God, do we remember that "Father" is also a metaphor? that God is *like* a loving father?

The exercise of reimaging God can be as liberating for men as for women, because the effort to use inclusive language goads us, pushes us, to ask ourselves: How and where do I experience God? How would I describe that divine activity in my own words as well as the words that tradition gives me?

Moses, at the burning bush, asked God to give him a name, *the* name, which Moses could then take as a sign of proof that God had indeed commissioned him to confront Pharaoh. God answers: "I am who I am, I will be who I will be." It sounds like God is being evasive, but as Carter Heyward reminds us, "God is warning us that we had best not try to find our security in any well-defined concept or category of what is Godly—for the minute we believe we are into God, God is off again and calling us forth into some unknown place."[5]

Feminists and other liberation theologians are lifting up new and old images that can give us new glimpses into the divine reality—images like: shalom of our being, womb of life, shelter for the homeless, mother *and* father, lover, friend, liberator of the oppressed. These images challenge the false equations that too many of us have been taught: that God is everything we are not; that we can come closer to God only by distancing from our bodies and our humanity.

The teacher, advocate, and friend whom Mary Magdalene, Joanna, and Mary witnessed to that Easter morning affirmed the preciousness, worth, and dignity of every human being. Jesus also saw the smallness, cruelty, and mean-spiritedness of people. He knew that sin, evil, and alienation are the result of humanity's wrong choices just as he knew that peace, love, and justice are the result of humanity's right choices. We have the power to choose. Sin is not being human; sin is failing to be *fully* human. Sin is alienation. It is the breaking up, the breaking down, the tearing asunder of relatedness in such forms of dominance and submission as sexism, racism, homophobia, or abuse of the environment. Faith is the recovery of our power to live in relationship, to mend and heal the broken places, to work for justice—which means literally, *right relation.*

How we understand and image God has everything to do with how we understand and image ourselves, each other, and the earth. In this *kairos* time, women and men are claiming the power to do our own imaging, seeking God among the living and asking: Where is this new blossom that is breaking from the bud? In this *kairos* moment, we are invited to venture into unknown places. We cannot know, beforehand, what we will find; what "new, hidden things" will be revealed. We can, however, trust that wherever justice is increased and the dignity of every person affirmed, these new things are of God.

12

S O P H I A ' S   F R I E N D S

In each generation, [Sophia]
passes into holy souls,
she makes them friends of God and prophets. . . .
—WISDOM 7:27B *(THE JERUSALEM BIBLE)*

Sophia, Holy Wisdom of God, I want to walk with you, listen to you, learn from you, lean into you, trust myself to you so that you might reveal your secrets to me.

I have been privileged to meet you in some of the people whom you call your children, your prophets and friends. I am grateful to have known wise women and men like Carol Putnam, Ludrell Pope, Dora Anderson, and Tine Kamphuis. For I have seen you, Sophia, in those

who know how to wait
who are relaxed but not resigned
who know their shadow side
who have known forgiveness
who have tender hearts
who possess revolutionary patience
who limp from wrestling in the night
who see to the heart of the matter
who can discern the times and seasons, knowing when to speak and when to be silent, when to embrace and when to let go.

who don't push the river and yet don't settle for the way
things are
who know things are not always as they seem
who reverence life
who understand that each of us must find her own truth
who know they will die
who believe that nothing, absolutely nothing, can separate
them from the love of God
who trust their intuition and speak in their own voice
who know that God has many names
who have learned from suffering
who recognize the holiness of certain moments and
encounters
who know how to comfort others
who allow others to change
who have a knowing, playful twinkle in their eyes
who have experienced oppression and have tasted
liberation
who hope for things unseen and do not cease to dream
who do not think of themselves as wise.

III

RESURRECTION

STORIES

13

RISING LIKE THE
PHOENIX

A New Church Movement

In 1988, the Holy Spirit was at work in different regions of America's heartland, stirring things up, bringing people together, descending like a dove and ascending like a phoenix.

Unbeknownst to each other, within months of each other, three new congregations were being born—Phoenix Community Church in Kalamazoo, Michigan; Spirit of the Lakes in Minneapolis, Minnesota; and Grace Baptist in Chicago, Illinois. These new congregations were not the result of denominational planning, demographic studies, or new church funds. No one could have predicted them. Yet that is the biblical witness to how the Spirit moves; sometimes, without precedent, the Spirit moves across rigid boundaries, making a way in the wilderness and rivers in the desert.

It has happened before—at times when the Spirit surprised and disrupted the officially adopted church growth programs. It happened when Philip baptized a man who was considered, as a gentile eunuch, to be sexually abnormal and outside the faith community. It happened when Peter followed his heart which told him to listen to a dream and, flying in the face of tradition and scripture, he baptized uncircumcised gentiles. When Peter was called by the

This essay is adapted from an address delivered at a conference on evangelism and church growth held at Chicago Theological Seminary, Chicago, Illinois.

church elders to defend his actions he said, "If God wishes to give them the same gift that God gave us, who am I to stand in the way of the Spirit of God?" It happened when Christians worked for the abolition of slavery. It happened in the mid-1800s, when the first woman was ordained to the ministry—Antoinette Brown. It happened with the development of the Metropolitan Community Churches in the late 1960s. It happened as established churches joined programs such as the More Light Churches Network in the 1970s and early 1980s.

It was happening again in 1988 in Kalamazoo, in Minneapolis, in Chicago, as lesbians and gay men gathered in living rooms to plan and dream and envision new church communities that would be welcoming and hospitable places for people who had experienced the world as unsafe and the church as the least safe place of all.

We are talking about church growth here, evangelism, the revival of hearts, the moving of the Spirit. We are talking about gathering in women and men who have not dared to walk through a church door for ten, twenty, thirty years, since they left their churches of origin after hearing once too often that they were sinners and their expression of love an abomination. We are talking about evangelism with the unchurched or, better said, the dischurched.

In these new churches—and since 1988 many more have sprung up—powerful stories of resurrection are being told and heard: persons confronting fear and learning to act and speak with increasing boldness, even when they are afraid. Stories are told of people who have experienced the deadness of silence and invisibility and yet responded to the challenge to come out, to choose life, to leave the grave and the closet behind, and to join the community of faith again.

The story I know best, of course, is the story of Phoenix Community Church in Kalamazoo. In October 1987, my friend and colleague Cyril Colonius was forced to leave the congregation he had served for six years solely because he is gay. In the aftermath of that dismissal, I suggested to Cyril that the time had come for us to start a "base" community that would be truly welcoming and liberating for all people, including lesbians and gay men.

On Ash Wednesday evening, February 17, 1988, eighteen people gathered in Cyril's living room in Kalamazoo to begin conversation about forming a new congregation. We chose the name Phoenix Community Church as a symbol of the hope that gave birth to this church. The phoenix is a mythological bird that rises out of its own ashes to new life. This Egyptian myth was appropriated by the early Christian church as a symbol of resurrection. We who gathered in Kalamazoo also appropriated this myth as a symbol of our belief that resurrection is possible out of the ashes of discrimination and oppression. We set out on a journey together believing that hope, like a phoenix, could rise again in us and that God could renew our strength and set us flying.

Resurrection continues to be a central theme at Phoenix. On Easter each year, people are invited to share their own personal stories of death and resurrection. Coming-out stories are told, stories of recovery from chemical dependency or abuse, and stories of new life after a time of despair or self-hatred.

Phoenix and other new church communities are not only about the task of creating welcoming congregations for lesbians and gay men, but also are committed to liberation theology, to making the links between racism, sexism, ableism, and heterosexism.

The real-life experience of being an exile can lay the foundations for liberating, welcoming faith communities. Such was the wisdom of the ancient prophets who reminded Israel to welcome the stranger and the sojourner because "you know what it is to be a stranger and a sojourner in Egypt." We give more than lip service to hospitality at Phoenix because we know what it is to be a stranger, an exile, and to be invisible within many churches. We know how it feels not to hear our true name spoken in a church or have our experiences validated as real and normal. Therefore, braille bulletins are available at Phoenix, and we avoid language—either spoken or sung—that is hurtful or excluding.

The apostle Paul's declaration that "In Christ there is neither male nor female, Jew nor Gentile, slave nor free" was a liberating message that proclaimed equality and justice. However, the proclamation that we are all one can sometimes blur our differences and serve to reinforce the norms of the majority. Thus, in our church communities, we might rephrase Paul's declaration by saying, "In Christ, there is male *and* female; old *and* young; disabled *and* temporarily able-bodied; lesbian, gay, *and* heterosexual." We celebrate the fact that each of us has particular gifts for ministry and mission not in spite of, but because of, our particular sex, age, race, orientation, and abilities.

We are seeking new theological "wineskins" that can adequately hold and convey the good news of God's love and justice for our day; that can recover the old language and imagery when it is life giving and can convey to people in our times the heart of the message. Members of churches such as Phoenix Community Church are particularly sensitive to how the Christian tradition has been used to reinforce self-contempt and judgment of others. As a minority that has been labeled as "sinners" and targeted by a heterosexist culture as the embodiment of the Fall, we are keenly aware how damaging and destructive the doctrine of "original sin" can be. Therefore, when we introduce the Prayer of Confession in our worship service, we speak of it as the invitation to "tell the truth about our lives." The good news of "original grace" is preached at Phoenix, along with the assurance that nothing, absolutely nothing— not the threat of violence nor the taunts of bigots nor our own internalized fear and self-contempt—will be able to separate us from the love of God.

We decided in 1990 to seek affiliation with the United Church of Christ. Toward the end of that year-long process, as the vote about Phoenix was nearing, four meetings were held at different locations so that members of local United Church of Christ churches could come to hear the Phoenix story and meet Phoenix members.

I felt intense pride as members of Phoenix got up before an audience of strangers and vulnerably told their stories of how they had left the churches of their childhood and youth because they could not believe what they were being told, because they were not seen as whole and equal persons by virtue of gender or sexual orientation or abilities. They told how they had almost given up hope of ever finding a church home when someone told them about Phoenix Community Church. They witnessed to their faith rebirthed, to their experience of worship being like a homecoming because they could be themselves without fear or shame. They invited members of other United Church of Christ churches to join with Phoenix in our ministry and mission, to support us, nurture us, challenge us, and say "yes" with us to what the Spirit is doing in our midst.

I felt pride when members of other churches said to me, "I can't imagine being able to give such a personal testimony about my faith and my local church!" I felt joy that myths, fears, and stereotypes were being shattered by this encounter between flesh-and-blood human beings. I felt hope, knowing that no matter how the vote went, this too was evangelism, this too was church growth. The wider church was being stretched and pushed into new places, and we at Phoenix were experiencing community with other church people.

Of course, I also felt sadness when ugly remarks were made, when our motives were impugned, when the Bible was used as a weapon. I felt protectiveness for my people—fearful that we might have to endure one more rejection at the hands of a church. And I wondered to myself what I would do if we were not accepted.

People in other churches asked, "Why do you find it necessary to start a new congregation? Why not work within existing congregations to make them more open?" Our response was, "That is important work. You do it! But those of us who are lesbian and gay can't wait any longer. There has already been too much lost: too many stories unshared, too many closets, too many lives broken, too many secrets and lies, too much silence and invisibility. We must have alternatives *now* to funeral services where gay or lesbian people are eulogized and their partner of fifteen years sits in the front row and is never mentioned! We need a church community that dares to do a new thing . . . and we need a spiritual home where we tell our stories now, sing our songs now, celebrate our relationships now, affirm ourselves now, use inclusive language for God now . . . not later, not sometime."

In April 1991, delegates from churches in southwest Michigan gathered to vote on whether to accept Phoenix Community Church into the United Church of Christ. An amazing thing happened that day: one by one, members of local churches rose and came to the microphone and told their own stories, made their own testimonials about meeting Phoenix people and about worshiping at Phoenix. One pastor of a small-town church said that he had been very skeptical until he and his wife had attended worship at Phoenix and he had experienced the Holy Spirit moving there as he had seldom known it in worship. He said, "I would be honored to be in partnership with this spirit-filled people." There were also those who spoke against our affiliation. But when the vote was taken, ninety-two people voted for and twenty-nine against the inclusion of Phoenix into the United Church of Christ.

In June of 1991, more than two hundred people gathered for a covenant service to welcome Phoenix Community Church into the United Church of Christ. We read from the fifty-sixth chapter of Isaiah, where the prophet proclaims that God will not be bound by human barriers or prejudice. God will do the calling and the welcoming. This chapter from Isaiah proclaims divine blessing to sexual minorities who were excluded from full membership in the worshiping community.[1] To the eunuch who cannot bear children in a society where "be fruitful and multiply" was considered a religious duty, God will give an everlasting name that not even death will blot out. God welcomes all people who keep the covenant: "for my house shall be a house of prayer for *all* peoples. . . . I will gather others to them besides those already gathered"(Isa. 56:7–8).

During the covenant service—which was alive with dancing, singing, storytelling, laughter and tears—one person after another rose to tell a story of coming home after being church-homeless for years. A Unitarian Universalist minister came to the microphone and explained how he had hoped Phoenix might choose to affiliate with the Unitarians: "But sitting in this service I have come to understand that that would not have been the right choice. There is a wound in the body of Christ," he said, "a wound that needs to be healed, and this day we are witnessing the healing."

When those ninety-two women and men from local congregations in southwest Michigan voted to extend standing to Phoenix Community Church, they were not only doing something ground-breaking for an American Protestant denomination. They were also helping to fulfill the vision of God's dream, a dream that the prophet glimpsed centuries ago. Until those considered outcasts are gathered in, neither can there be full joy on the holy mountain nor can our churches truly be called houses of prayer.

14

A HUMAN BEING
FULLY ALIVE

I will never forget listening to an Easter sermon during the first year of my stay in the Netherlands. Struggling as I was with the Dutch language, much of the sermon escaped me. My grammar and vocabulary were still so limited that I was responding in a fashion typical to most foreigners: Why do these people talk so much more rapidly than English-speakers? I had the sensation of furiously swimming against a current of unknown nouns and verbs, trying to stay abreast of those around me who appeared to float effortlessly with the stream.

One new word in particular was repeated so frequently I assumed it to be a main thread with which the preacher was weaving this Easter tapestry of a sermon. So I forsook my pride and asked the Dutch woman seated next to me: "What is that word *opstanding?*" She closed her eyes, searching to retrieve the English equivalent from the pages of her mental dictionary.

"Resurrection!" she whispered with a smile and a triumphant tone (the Dutch are exasperatingly fluent in foreign languages).

"*Opstanding, opstanding . . .*" I said the word over and over to myself while the remainder of the sermon flowed on. To my untrained ear, this word sounded as though it meant "standing up." After the service, I pursued the matter further with my obviously articulate neighbor.

"Standing up?" I asked, "Is that what resurrection means in Dutch?"

Looking somewhat puzzled and caught off guard by my much-too-literal translation, she responded, "Well, sort of. Don't you say something similar in English? 'To rise up?' Don't you say that Jesus 'rose from the dead?'"

Now I was the one who was perplexed: of course that's what we say, but it sounds so different. Resurrection—the act of standing up. Perhaps when words like "resurrection" become theological doctrines of the church, there is a danger that we hear them as concepts, abstractions that have taken on a static quality. The encounter with the Dutch word "opstanding" helped me see and hear again the dynamic, verbal quality of resurrection as an event rather than a concept: resurrection means standing up out of death to life.

Suddenly I realized that this dynamic—this standing up from death to life—is found not only in the Easter narratives but throughout the gospels.

Jesus was continually calling people to arise, to stand up, to actively forsake the ways of death and choose life. Time and again, we hear this resurrection challenge in the healing narratives, in the calling of the disciples, and in his parables.

The man with paralysis was told to stand up, to take up his bed and walk. When Jesus passed by the tax office where Matthew was working, Matthew's response to the call to discipleship is portrayed in two simple verbs: he *stood up* and *followed* Jesus. And the prodigal son, lying in the deathlike stench of the swine, came to himself and said: "I will stand up (arise) and go to my father."

Are not all of these, in some sense, resurrection accounts? And is this not what Jesus promised when he said, "I am the resurrection and the life"—that we may find new courage and new faith to stand up and choose life here and now? If the call to new life is a call to stand up and move on, then we can likewise understand death as inertia, staying put, holding on, sitting tight. Death, as the gospel narratives suggest, is the inability or unwillingness to move and change.

A resurrection faith not only looks beyond the grave to a time when we will be "raised in glory," it confesses that we are called to choose life on this side of the grave—to embrace wholeness and liberation and to give glory to God by becoming fully alive. As

Iraneus said so many centuries ago, "The glory of God is a human being fully alive."

One of the most poignant of all "resurrection accounts" is that of a woman who did just that—she stood up and gave God glory (Luke 13:10 17). She was present one Sabbath while Jesus was teaching in the synagogue. For eighteen years, this woman had been so bent over that as she walked, she saw only the ground under her and the feet of those she met. She seldom saw herself mirrored in the eyes of another. Her terrible, isolating illness relegated her to the margins of society: Who noticed her? Who took her into account and recognized what she had to give?

Someone in the synagogue that day recognized her. "Woman," he said in effect, "You are a daughter of Abraham. It is not your destiny to remain unnoticed and unheard." "Stand up," he told her, and he went to her and laid hands on her. Jesus tenderly touched this woman—something that most likely no one in all those eighteen years had done. And then, we are told, she stood up and praised God.

We are inclined to hear those two things—standing up and praising God—as distinct and separate, but they are one and the same. Praising God is not something the woman did afterward as a way of expressing her gratitude. Her act of standing up, of discovering her power and worth, her liberation from that which weighed her down—that *was* praising God, giving God glory. For the glory of God is a human being fully alive.

Not everyone rejoiced with this woman as she stood up. Not everyone present perceived that she was thereby giving God glory. In fact, her liberation constituted a threat to someone else. It shook the foundation of the religious convictions of the synagogue elder. Sensing an approaching chaos unless such disturbances were stopped, he stepped forward and reprimanded Jesus, essentially saying, "Look, this sort of thing shouldn't be happening on the Sabbath. There are six days in which you're free to carry on like this—but not on the Sabbath and not here!"

Jesus reacted with nothing short of rage. He called the synagogue ruler a hypocrite and then said in effect, "What are you telling me? Is it impossible for you to be happy that this woman has been set free? Does she mean less to you than your donkey, to which you give water on the Sabbath? She is a human being, a beloved child of God. She is a daughter of Abraham—and that means a sister of yours. She has responded to the call to stand up and choose life. Nothing fulfills the Sabbath more than that. If God cannot be praised on the Sabbath, when can God be praised?"

This brief episode in the gospel of Luke contains powerful resurrection imagery. Against all odds and expectations, a human being comes to new life. Having been touched by someone who believes in her, she finds the courage to believe in herself and claim her full humanity. With dignity and joy, with arms outstretched to give and receive, she raises her voice in praise.

If we are to hear this episode as a resurrection story, then we must avoid a too-narrowly literal reading of this healing, which might insult persons with physical illnesses or handicaps. It is not the literal act of standing that makes this story a resurrection account. It is the woman's response to the call to liberation and new life. Like the woman in the synagogue, those who are physically challenged in our society are demanding to be seen and heard for who they are. They are rejecting ableist norms and definitions of what constitutes physical beauty and wholeness, and they are also calling all of us to examine the ways that ableism has functioned to oppress them.

Newfound freedom for some people often occasions fear in others. The bold act of the woman in the synagogue claiming her full humanity sent shock waves through those who want things nailed down and secure, who wanted order restored and cherished traditions and values held intact. The drama of this confrontation cannot be safely or smugly dismissed as antiquated; the story is powerful and disturbing precisely because it brings to mind events and experiences quite close to home.

Each of us, at one time or another, has felt something akin to this woman's pain and joy. All of us have struggled to free ourselves from burdens that threatened to crush our spirits—burdens such as others' expectations that we cannot fulfill, or hurts, disappointments, prejudices, and accusations. And I suspect that we have all felt something akin to the threat, fear, and anger that the ruler of the synagogue felt as we see people close to us change and grow, disrupting familiar patterns and surprising us with unsettling revelations and behavior.

This resurrection theme is seen in many real-life occurrences. For example, we see it in the woman who for years has held her own dreams in abeyance for the sake of her husband and children. When she one day decides to pursue those dreams, her new behavior disrupts the firmly established patterns of family interactions and her husband initially feels deprived and angry. Then there is the gay man who for years tried to hide his sexual orientation from his family and friends until one day he decides he is not ashamed or afraid to declare openly his love for another man. As he stands upright, rejoicing in the gift of that love, he meets with shock, fear, and rejection from those who feel he is threatening the "good order." We also see a spirit of resurrection in the blind woman who has attended church for years, sitting silently while the rest of the congregation says responsive prayers and sings hymns. One day she decides to speak out and let the congregation know that they are not as welcoming as they claim to be. Without braille bulletins, entrance ramps for wheelchairs, and signers for the deaf, the congregation has excluded people with disabilities. Her speaking out and naming injustice are met with protestations on the part of some church members who feel defensive or who question whether the church budget can accommodate everyone.

As I reflect on this story from Luke's gospel and the experiences it brings to mind, I find myself wondering: Is it inevitable that one person's liberation constitutes another person's threat? As one person comes into his or her own, does this process always evoke resistance and opposition in others?

Such conflict seems almost inevitable. Yet that need not occasion despair or resignation. Perhaps, after all, Jesus' words made a deep impression on the synagogue ruler; perhaps something broke open in him and he was able to recognize this woman for who she was—his sister, a daughter of Abraham and Sarah, a human being who had stood up from death to new life. In such a case, this man could have discovered something more of his own humanity: he, too, would have tasted the resurrection that was at the heart of Jesus' mission.

The gospels make it clear that Jesus is grieved when people such as this woman live burdened, isolated lives, out of touch with themselves and others. Equally clear is Jesus' rage with religious people who, for the sake of maintaining order or defending scriptural authority, stand in the way of persons claiming their full humanity. He expects, at the very least, that his followers will not obstruct the liberating work of God. To do so is to miss the power of resurrection.

15

REMEMBERING

RE-IMAGINING

In mid-May 1994, two friends living in different locations called to tell me that they had heard my voice on Pat Robertson's television program, *The 700 Club*. The callers explained that they had been "channel surfing" when they heard a familiar voice on a most unexpected network. Apparently Robertson was broadcasting a statement I had made months earlier at the Re-Imagining Conference.

In November 1993, approximately two thousand women and one hundred men attended the Re-Imagining Conference in Minneapolis, sponsored by a coalition of churches in recognition of the World Council of Churches' "Ecumenical Decade: Churches in Solidarity with Women." Organizers of the event invited participants to engage in a reimagining process to expand traditional understandings of spirituality and theology, because, as they said, "some ways of doing theology have been costly to creation, and to our relationships with each other, ourselves, and our God."[1]

Feminist theologians from many countries and many cultures addressed the conference, bringing joy and renewal to most of the participants. Others, hearing of what went on in Minneapolis, reacted with dismay and anger, organizing campaigns within their denominations to withhold funds in protest and to discipline national staff members involved in planning the conference. An inquisitional atmosphere has surfaced in some places, with candidates for ordination being asked if they attended the Re-Imagining Conference. Retired United Methodist Bishop Earl G. Hunt said of certain aspects of the conference, "No comparable heresy has appeared in the church in the last fifteen centuries."[2]

I don't know the exact nature of Pat Robertson's commentary on the conference. Based on other segments of *The 700 Club* that I've seen, I can wager a guess. The clip of tape he played was from the conference's Saturday morning plenary session. I was not a scheduled speaker for Saturday morning; my name was not in the program. How I came to stand on the speaker's platform that day is a story I want to share.

The racial and ethnic diversity of the presenters at the Re-Imagining Conference was breathtaking. Leadership for the workshops was also hearteningly diverse in terms of race, religious background, and sexual orientation. Nevertheless, some of us among the participants who are lesbian began to grow uneasy because when all two thousand participants gathered for presentations, no one was speaking in a lesbian voice.

Afternoon presentations and workshops had an out-lesbian presence, but afternoon events were optional. Although we learned that one of the plenary presenters planned to make a strong and personal coming-out statement at the closing worship service, we felt that there should be lesbian voice and visibility before that time. After all, this was an ecumenical gathering with representatives from many denominations, most of which have repressive policies and statements regarding lesbian women. We felt that no one should leave a conference highlighting the "Ecumenical Decade: Churches in Solidarity with Women" without having to wrestle directly with the question of what it means to be in solidarity with lesbian women.

Fearing that this question otherwise might not be raised when all of us were gathered, we decided to approach the conference steering committee and ask for time to make a brief statement during Saturday morning's plenary session. After much negotiation, the conference planners agreed to give us a few minutes to make an unofficial statement.

As cochair of the coordinating council of CLOUT (Christian Lesbians OUT Together), I was selected to invite, from center stage, all lesbian, bisexual, and transsexual women to circle the platform and sing, celebrating our courage. Only a handful of us knew what was going to happen that Saturday morning. We hoped that enough women would come forward to complete a circle around the stage, but we couldn't be certain. We knew that for many women—clergy and lay—it could very risky to come out in front of members of their denomination, who could then go home and tell their bishops or others with power over them.

I introduced myself and explained that I work with CLOUT, an ecumenical movement celebrating the miracle of being lesbian, out, and Christian. I then said, "We are keenly, painfully aware that the world is not safe for lesbian women and that often the *least* safe place is the church. We call upon all of you—whatever your sexual orientation—not to leave this holy place without wrestling with these questions: what does it mean for us to be in solidarity with lesbian, bisexual, and transsexual women in this decade, and how can we together reimagine our churches so that *every* woman may claim her voice, her gifts, her loves, and her wholeness? Acknowledging that my white skin may put me in a place where there is less at stake in coming out, I invite every lesbian, bisexual, and transsexual woman who is willing and able to come forward and join hands, encircling this platform, facing out."

As soon as I issued the invitation, women in every part of that great hall left their tables and started moving toward the center of the room. At least 150 women circled the stage, three rows deep and spilling up onto the platform. I intended to ask the people remaining at their tables to stand in solidarity with us. But when women began to stream to the center, a roar went up from the crowd as people rose spontaneously to their feet and gave the women a long and thunderous ovation. It was glorious pandemonium. From the platform, I could see tears running down the faces of many who stood at their tables. People were cheering and waving their arms. The women who circled the stage faced the cheering people, clasping each other's hands and raising their arms in a triumphant gesture of pride and strength.

I reminded everyone that there were women standing at their tables who wanted to be in this circle but who did not yet feel safe enough to join us. We sang, "We're going to keep on moving forward, we're going to keep on speaking truthfully, we're going to keep on loving women, we're going to work for change together . . . never turning back, never turning back."[3] And then the room erupted in more applause, hugs, and tears.

During the remainder of the conference, woman after woman approached us to tell how she experienced what happened Saturday morning. Some said that this was the first time they had ever dared to come out in such a public way. Others said they did not feel safe enough to join us, but they felt supported and affirmed by the action and the applause.

Many straight women sought us out to say that they were deeply appreciative that this challenge had been issued and tangibly enacted in such a compelling way. "What you all did," one woman said, "was the most powerful moment in a very empowering conference." We also heard many testimonies about how our act of vulnerable courage broke open conversation at the tables in a new way.

I suspect that none of us who planned this event on Saturday morning dared dream that the support would be so dramatic and demonstrable. But it seems that the time was right to name the wound in the body of Christ. The cathartic power of what erupted that Saturday morning signifies how much the church has suffered from enforced closets and threats of expulsion. The eruption also testifies to the tenacious, indefatigable spirit of healing that returns when individuals refuse to collude with fear any longer.

Standing on the stage, I knew that nothing could ever kill the memory of that grace-filled moment. That memory has carried me through some frightening times since, when I've been face to face with people who insist that lesbians and gay men—not heterosexism and homophobia—are purveyors of division and disease within the church. In the aftermath of that Saturday morning, when campaigns were launched to discredit the conference and divide participants from one another by fanning the flames of homophobia, I have been sustained by the memory of that moment when courage and solidarity were so palpable.

The attacks on the Re-Imagining Conference include a variety of charges and caricatures, but blatant homophobia runs through them all. The front of a fund-raising envelope included in the *Presbyterian Layman* is just one of many examples. It reads:

> *"Did you want*
>
> - *your Presbyterian church money spent on a conference to worship the female goddess "Sophia"?*
> - *your Presbyterian National Staff planning a conference where leaders rejected the atonement of Jesus Christ, celebrated lesbianism and called for adding books to the Bible that could then be used to justify radical feminist and homosexual activism?*
> - *your Presbyterian National Staff participating in a pagan worship ritual?"*

Rumor has it that some conservative groups are scanning photographs of this Saturday morning event, hoping to identify particular women. I was moved to tears when I heard the response of one Lutheran heterosexual sister who said, "If that happens, then those of us who are heterosexual will have to step forward and say, 'I was there! I was in that circle! Didn't you see me? Maybe you can't see me in that photo, but I was there!'"

On hearing that Pat Robertson was playing the tape of my voice on *The 700 Club,* I felt a mixture of fear and rage. I could hardly bear the thought of his attempts to profane such a holy moment. Then a friend told me how he had been giving thanks for the fact that God was using even Pat Robertson to get the message out to lesbian women. When I realized he wasn't joking, my fear and rage were transformed into delight and gratitude. For surely lesbian women who have been taught to despise themselves watch *The 700 Club.* And some of them might have been warmed and encouraged by hearing the thunderous applause that surrounded the lesbian women at the Re-Imagining Conference. Perhaps they heard, via Pat Robertson, that they have a community of sisters and brothers waiting to receive them as they come out and come home. Wouldn't that give new meaning to the old expression that God moves in mysterious ways Her wonders to perform!

16

WHAT WE CAN
(AND CANNOT)
DO FOR ONE ANOTHER

The first time I ever preached about Lazarus rising from the dead was at the wedding of two close friends in the Netherlands: Jim and Nancy. It may seem strange to choose for a wedding sermon a text more commonly read at funerals, a story with so many tears, so much pain and grieving. Yet it is a story about life every bit as much as death, and about the power of love that can bring us from death to life.

Jim and Nancy chose this story for their wedding because both had been previously married. The end of Jim's first marriage had grieved him terribly. "I walked through life as a man half dead," he told me as we were preparing for the service. "Death had the upper hand for a long time and it seemed as though the season of grieving would never end. The gradual blossoming of an old friendship into love was a resurrectionlike experience that made me identify with Lazarus being called out of the tomb. This gradual warming brought about by correspondence made me capable of receiving the love Nancy offered me. So this time around, the gratitude is deeper. Loving again after feeling so cut off fills me with gratitude."

Just before Nancy arrived in the Netherlands, Jim wrote me: "Nancy arrives in just a few more days. It's not quite excitement I feel. Gratitude, really, such immense gratitude. . . . I remember a movie in which Jack Lemmon keeps saying, within his thoughts,

'Thank you, God, amen.' It was like his own inner Greek chorus, and I thought, now that's a very good prayer."

Jim's story, like Lazarus', was a resurrection story. Both were about a person hearing and answering the call to choose life. Too often Lazarus has been pictured as a passive recipient; a man who has a miracle performed *on* him, as though he had no part in it. Such a reading of the story is unjust not only to Lazarus but also to Jesus, because it makes Jesus appear to be a mere magician who does amazing things like make bodies rise. Actually, Lazarus is confronted with a choice: he is called to come out and join the community again. He, and only he, can answer this call.

But we're jumping ahead to the end of the story. Let's go back to where Jesus approaches the city of Bethany. Although Lazarus had been dead for four days, a community of friends was still gathered around his sisters, Martha and Mary. They were "sitting shiva," the Jewish mourning ritual still practiced today. The immediate family of the deceased stay together for seven days, saying Kaddish (the Mourners' Prayer) every morning and refraining from any work.

Friends of Mary and Martha were sitting with them, weeping with them and most likely reminiscing about Lazarus, the way we do when someone we love dies: "You remember how he could laugh with abandon, throwing his head back? He was always there for other people. Did I tell him recently enough that I loved him?"

Having heard that Jesus was approaching the city, Martha left this group of mourners to meet Jesus at the edge of the city, presumably so that she could talk with him alone. "Oh, Jesus," she said, "if only you had been here, my brother would not have died."

"Your brother will rise again," Jesus responded.

Martha seemed to understand what Jesus meant: "I know that he will rise again in the resurrection at the last day." But that was not what Jesus meant. He was not talking about some future event. Here and now, he said, death has been disarmed. Its power has been conquered and broken. It may not appear to be so; it may appear that death has the upper hand and that life and love are fragile, powerless, and fleeting. But, Jesus explained, faith means knowing that whether we live or die nothing can separate us from the Eternal, not even death.

Mary, hearing that Jesus was outside the city, also went to him. Her friends went with her for support, thinking that she was going to the grave. When Jesus saw Mary and her friends weeping, he was deeply moved, and he asked, "Where have you laid him?"

"Come and see," they replied. But Jesus didn't move in the direction of the grave; he stood there and wept. He wept. Grief overtook him, and he let it come. He didn't hold back the tears or hide them. He didn't say, "Not to worry folks! Stop your weeping! I'm about to perform a miracle that will dazzle you and make everything okay." Nor did he say, "Why are you sad? Don't you know that Lazarus is now with God?" No, he stood there and wept. And the others whispered, "See how much he loved Lazarus."

It is very important that *we* also stop and stand there, taking this moment in, allowing ourselves to feel the helplessness and grief of that circle of mourners before we rush on to the conclusion of the story. We may recognize the helplessness and grief we, too, have felt when we suffer in love for and with another person. That kind of helplessness is not restricted to grief at the literal death of someone we love any more than the experience of death is restricted to literal, physical death.

While in the Netherlands, I received a letter from a friend whose son had suffered a great personal loss. This loss had caused him to turn inward, away from others. He had come to stay for a while in his parent's home; but aside from saying "good morning" and "good night," he spoke very little, refusing to talk about his feelings. He didn't smile, laugh, or cry. It was as though he were unable or unwilling to feel anymore.

His mother, my friend, was in great pain, because he held her at a distance, walking around the house like a man dead to himself and others. "I feel so helpless to reach him," she wrote to me, "I suffer so much with him and I want to hold him, to let him know he is not alone, and that he is very much loved, but he won't let me in. There is nothing I can do but wait with him, however long it takes, and when he is able to touch or be touched again—to let others come close again—I will be there."

Like the friends gathered to mourn Lazarus or like this patient mother, we can feel so helpless in knowing that, as much as we want

to, we cannot bring a friend or loved one back from death to life.
Like Lazarus and my friend's son, we may have experienced times of
death ourselves—times when we simply could not risk feeling anything anymore because the pain was too overwhelming, when we
walked through life doing what we had to do but feeling frozen
inside, when we were unable to touch one another because our arms
were tightly wrapped in our shrouds of fear.

Such times may have been caused by great loss, by bitter disappointment, or by the end of relationships we believed would never
end. We feel broken, shattered, cold. We see and hear our friends
trying to comfort us; but their words, their presence, their gestures
of comfort and love cannot reach us. We are cut off, trapped behind
barriers as immovable as a gravestone; and neither our own strength
alone nor the combined strengths of our friends can roll the stone
away.

Those times when we are unreachable are something like being dead. However many days, weeks, or years they last feel like an
eternity because there seems no hope of change.

But then . . . how can we explain it? How will we ever find
the words to describe how it happens that we are touched again,
called to choose life again, called to come out of the shadows into
the light. We could call such moments experiences of *resurrection*. It
is so difficult to say exactly how we reach that turning point, even
though we know when we experience it. Often, such times of
resurrection are mediated by another person who has waited for us
in love. They can also be mediated by music, books, or something
we glimpse in nature that fills us with awe.

However it happens, we experience being called by name,
being held and upheld, loved. I would describe that kind of experience in my own life as an experience of God's presence, because I
sensed that the source of life itself has taken hold of me again, shaken
me, called me to come out of the grave. And as I do, I am aware that
that source of life and love (which I call God) was there all along. It
never let me go. That spirit of life and love held me, sought me, even
when I could not feel it or hear it or let it in.

In such resurrection moments, we are confronted with a decision: to stay in the grave or to choose the path of healing, taking

hold of what has already taken hold of us. Lazarus was confronted with this decision in the loud cry from Jesus: "Come out."

When we stand on faltering legs that have been wrapped in hopelessness and we walk toward others again, we are still trailing the grave clothes, still partially bound by them. We wonder if it is a dream, if we can really trust in life again.

Lazarus appeared with his hands and feet still bound with bandages, his face wrapped with a cloth. Jesus turned to the community of friends and said, "Unbind him and let him go." In other words, "Help him know that it is not a dream, help him believe that he is in fact alive again, that he can love again. Touch him, unwrap the fears that bind him, get close enough to touch his pain, and assure him that he can go on living, trusting in this new life."

What this story so subtly and profoundly describes is what we *can* and what we *cannot* do for one another. We cannot save each other. We cannot bring another person from death to life. If a person chooses to persist in self-destructive behavior, we cannot force or cajole or plead that person out of that behavior. If we see a friend stuck in self-defeating patterns, we can point this out, as a friend may do; but we *cannot* do the hard work of healing for another person.

What we can do is wait with one another, waiting on God, believing in the transforming power of love. We can wait and pray and remind one another that nothing can separate us from the love of God—not self-hatred, shame, terrifying memories, or the fear that we will never get through the pain. Nothing, absolutely nothing, can separate us from this love.

We can also be there to receive the other person when he or she takes the steps that only she or he can take. We can be there, not to smother or coerce but, if asked, to help unwrap the doubts and fears that bind our friend. We can do this not from a position of superiority but only from an acknowledgment of our own woundedness and need for healing. And we cannot do this unless we are invited to do so; an uninvited touch is intrusive. "Unbind him and let him go" is an invitation, an awesome privilege and responsibility. It is an invitation to believe in original grace and to encourage one another to heal. It is an invitation to announce by our words, our presence, and our own stories of healing that we believe in original grace because we believe there is a divine source of life and love that held us, sought us, never let us go.

When Lazarus heard the invitation to come out and join the community again, he was faced with a choice. Jesus did not perform magic, raising Lazarus against his will; rather, he issued an invitation—albeit a confrontive, challenging invitation—for Lazarus to live again and love again. However, it was Lazarus himself who had to do the rising, the walking, the believing, the healing.

When I say we are confronted with a choice whether to stay in the grave or to come out, I do not mean to speak naively as though that choice were only a matter of willpower. I do not mean to leave the impression that those who cannot make that choice are less courageous or less faithful. Some people have experienced such hurt or abuse or pain that the struggle to stay alive is too hard, and no amount of love or support or waiting can pull them through. I firmly believe that the same source of life and love holds them and upholds them.

A church can be a community of persons who know both the limitations and the possibilities of human love because it is a community of persons who acknowledge the reality of divine love. We need the kind of community that waits with us, bears our pain with us, and celebrates with us even the most tentative steps out of the shadows of the grave into the light of love.

To experience the gift of love and the call to choose life after a time of brokenness is to know a boundless gratitude. For when we come out of the place of darkness, grief, and death into the midst of the community again and move toward that which is calling us to live again, we know we are loving not by our own strength alone but by the power of love—a love that even death could not destroy, a love that will not let us go.

17

A Time to Mourn
and a Time to Dance

Each September I am flooded with smells, sounds, and sights from childhood: leaves beginning to turn and fall; jumping in the pile of leaves my mother or father just neatly raked together; the distant drum roll of the Michigan State University marching band; the feel and look of new shoes; the conviction that the new notebook and row of sharpened pencils in my carrying case will mean good grades. September is a time of new beginnings.

September is also a time of endings. Despite September's beauty, its crisp mornings, its warm afternoon sun, and that peculiar slant of the sun through the trees, I find myself clutching the remnants of August, wanting to postpone the onslaught of autumn busyness. There is a sweet melancholy to September. Summer is over; the illusion that it would be restful is long gone. I use my calendar again in September. I make more lists. Life contains more demands and fewer escape routes.

The melancholy and the holding on signify more than the passing of summer and the changing of seasons. There is, subliminally at least, an awareness that another year is passing and that the life that breathes in my lungs and animates my body is fragile and tenuous. Even if life itself is not so fragile, our individual lives surely are. We know that the buds—with or without us—will appear again and the cycle of renewal will go on. But we grow older with each passing season, and there is nothing we can do to stop that process. My body is aging—irreversibly. When this knowledge is most acute, grief can overtake me. Sometimes anger, too. I cannot protect myself or the people I love against death. I remember how my father used to look at us when we were children with tenderness and joy. Then, suddenly, a look of dismay would also cross his face, and he would say, "I wish I could just freeze you in time, right like this, right as you are this moment." His delight in us was followed by the awareness that he could lose us, and everything in him resisted that thought.

The awareness of my own aging and the fleeting time that I have on this earth forces me to confront the question of what this life means and whether death is the end for me. I don't have many well-formulated answers to those questions, but I know what comforts me. The thought that life itself is greater than I am and my conviction that love is eternal and that the Eternal is love mean that I believe that somehow, in some form, in some way, we will be kept safe in that eternally loving presence.

Many people seem consoled by their belief that the spirit leaves the body at death and lives on. That image does not bring me solace. I am angry that death robs us of our embodied selves. The people I love and cherish are not just spirits to me. I love their bodies. I love their touch, their skin, their arms around me. As a woman in one of our Leaven seminars once said, "A friend is God with skin on." I don't want to say goodbye to the bodies of my friends and family and lover.

The poet in Ecclesiastes writes: "For everything, there is a season, and a time for every matter under heaven: A time to be born, and a time to die; a time to break down, and a time to build up; a time to mourn and a time to dance; a time to embrace, and a time to refrain from embracing."

This poem expresses the mystery of life and its rhythms: birth and death, holding on and letting go, dancing and mourning. Sometimes, however, this rhythm feels impossible, as though we are asked to do two contradictory things at once just by being alive. We are asked to embrace life boldly, not holding back and waiting to see the outcome. We are expected to give ourselves to life and other people in earnest commitment, investing ourselves, cherishing, and holding on. At the same time, we are asked to let go, to grieve, to mourn, to change, to uproot, and to break down. A deep protest can well up in me: Why can't it be one way or the other? If I am going to invest myself in love, in parenting, in friendship, in a church community, in dreams, why can't there be some guarantees? Why can't I be assured that this friend, this child, this lover, this community, this dream will not disappoint me, leave me, or die?

Some people play it safe, trying to avoid the hurt and disappointment. They hold people at arm's length, minimize their expectations, and suppress their capacity to dream. They may think they are thereby avoiding the season of weeping, letting go, breaking down, and mourning. In fact, they are also robbing themselves of the seasons of embracing, dancing, planting, and holding on. If we try to avoid one side of the rhythm, we won't be able to experience the other side. Unless we are able to grieve the losses, we won't be able to dance with abandon when that time comes. Getting stuck short of grieving stunts our capacity for joy. That's the mystery.

I am reminded of a woman who was a member of the first congregation my father served in the late 1940s and early 1950s. I will call her Rose Simpson. Toward the end of World War II, Rose and her husband received word that their oldest son, Larry, had been killed but his body had not been recovered. Even three years after the Simpsons learned of Larry's death, Rose still carried on her vigil. She wore black every day. She seldom left the house except to go to church or the grocery store, and she never went to social gatherings or parties. She held people at a distance, and her face was perpetually expressionless. Friends and family members, who had originally offered their condolences and tried to be available to Rose in her grief, found themselves at a loss to know what to do or say after so long a time.

People stopped visiting Rose or speaking to her directly, but they didn't stop talking about her. They said things like: "Someone ought to take Rose by the shoulders and shake her. It's been long enough now! She's neglecting her other children and her husband! We appreciate her pain and loss, but she's not the only person in the world to have lost a loved one. She needs to stop grieving and start enjoying life again!"

My father advised people not to say these things to Rose. He knew the problem wasn't that she couldn't stop grieving. Rose had never really started grieving. The black clothes and the never-ending vigil were her ways of holding everyone and everything—including grief—at a distance. Rose had not yet cried and screamed. She got stuck short of grieving. She couldn't enter the season of mourning and letting go, and therefore the season of dancing and laughing didn't return.

Another woman, who I will call Barbara, comes to see me every couple of weeks. She was ritually abused as a child—meaning that she was the victim of a Satanic cult in the small town where she grew up. The stories Barbara tells as she uncovers memories in her therapy are some of the most horrible, evil things I have ever heard. The work of remembering is incredibly painful. Sometimes she grabs hold of me and asks, "Why must I remember? Why must I grieve and go through this pain before I can come out on the other side?" I don't have answers. I do hear her protest. It isn't fair. It's just the way things are.

This September marks an ending and a new beginning in my life. Last Sunday, all the boxes and furniture were finally out of my old house and into the new. I have begun sharing my days and nights with my partner, April. I am very happy to make this transition. It's a time of planting, building up, embracing, and rejoicing. But right next to that season is the other season—so close that the seasons touch. I am also letting go, saying goodbye to five years of living alone, saying goodbye to my little house that has done so well in welcoming and sheltering me. I felt excitement packing the boxes. I also sat in the midst of the boxes and cried.

After April and I loaded everything into the car and stripped all the walls of pictures, we went back into the house and sat down together. We looked around and let ourselves feel what this house has been for each of us. It is where we got to know each other. It is also the house I found after returning from the Netherlands and starting all over again on this side of the ocean.

The grace of letting go is a difficult spiritual gesture but one that is asked of us again and again. I will never forget my mother telling me about visiting her friend Nancy who had given birth to her first child, a child she and her husband had been wanting for years. Amid the celebration, my mother noticed that Nancy was subdued. "Have you grieved yet?" my mother asked. "Grieved?" asked Nancy, whose eyes, wide with amazement, began to fill with tears. "What do I have to grieve? I have wanted this child forever."

"Yes," replied my mother. "But you also said goodbye to life as you have always known it. It will never be the same again. We don't just grieve for the things we dread. We sometimes have to grieve for the things we long for."

The grace to let go. On this September Sunday evening, another summer is past and another fall has begun. For everything there is a season, and a time for every matter under heaven. So be it.

18

L E T T E R   T O   A U D R E

On November 17, 1992, Audre Lorde died at the age of fifty-eight. She had been a poet, essayist, lecturer, teacher, and activist who had inspired women by her words for more than forty years. Her seventeen volumes of poetry and prose include Sister Outsider, Zami—A New Spelling of My Name, Our Dead Behind Us, Undersong, *and* The Cancer Journals. *In this letter, written a year after her death, I attempt to express what Audre Lorde has meant to me.*

November 1, 1993

Dear Audre:

I suppose it is fitting that I finish this letter to you in the season when we remember the saints. I began to write you months ago. The day I could finally cry—let go and feel that you are really gone. Something Margaret Randall wrote to you caused the tears to come: "Audre, everything seems more fragile since you're gone. . . . Suddenly I know the world is a more dangerous place, our lives are precarious, with you gone."[1] Until reading her words, I had been holding the tears in, pretending, resisting, afraid to feel how fragile things feel now.

Seven years ago, a wise friend put *Sister Outsider* in my hands, and my life has never been the same. My friend knew I was going into retreat—a year of solitude—to wrestle with the demons of fear that had kept me closeted. She said that if I was taking books with me into this retreat, then I must take yours. The first time I read

"The Transformation of Silence into Language" was like being hit in the stomach.

Your silence will not protect you.[2]

*In the cause of silence, each of us draws the face of her own
fear—fear of contempt, of censure, or some judgment, or recognition, of challenge, of annihilation. But most of all, I
think, we fear the visibility without which we cannot truly
live. . . . And that visibility which makes us most vulnerable
is that which also is the source of our greatest strength.*[3]

I was angry. How dare you rip away all my defenses? I put the book away, didn't even want to look at it, and let several weeks pass before I could touch it again. But your words haunted me and left me changed. More than any other single thing, confronting your words brought me out of the closet.

*We can learn to work and speak when we are afraid in the
same way we have learned to work and speak when we are
tired. For we have been socialized to respect fear more than
our own needs for language and definition, and while we wait
in silence for that final luxury of fearlessness, the weight of
that silence will choke us.*[4]

That's why, three years ago, after your speech in Ann Arbor, I stood in line for more than an hour, waiting to talk with you. I often feel disdain for groupies, but I needed to tell you face to face, woman to woman, what you have given me.

If I am packing for a trip and I can only take a couple books, *Sister Outsider* goes along. "The Blue Bible," I call it, because it is now unmistakably clear to me that the canon is not closed. *Sister Outsider* is one of the holy books. Whenever I quote from it, from the pulpit or elsewhere, I begin by saying, "Hear these words from the prophet Audre Lorde. . . ."

That night in Ann Arbor, you began your lecture by saying, "I am a black, lesbian, feminist, socialist, poet, lover, mother, warrior doing her work. . . .Who are you?"

Your question, "Who are you?" ripped into me. I had, by that

time, come out in the church as a lesbian. But I was tempted to hide
in a new closet. I was hesitant to acknowledge my identity as a
Christian or as an ordained minister to lesbians. Many lesbians who
long ago left the church because of its espousal of sexism and heterosexism are mystified that any self-respecting lesbian woman would
still be identified with Christianity.

When I heard you speak that night, I had just accepted an
invitation to address the Michigan Lesbian and Gay Pride March. I
was trying to write my speech without using "the C-word" (Christian) for fear of being discounted by the audience. But when you
asked, "Who are you?" I realized that I could only speak in my own
voice if I came out at the March, both as a lesbian *and* as a Christian.
My work as a Christian is profoundly influenced by my being a
lesbian, and my work as a lesbian is profoundly influenced by my
being a Christian.

Once again, Audre, your hard words broke open new possibilities. You asked, "Who are you?" and you asked that night as well,
"Are you willing to use the power that you have in the service of
what you say you believe in?"

So, on those Capitol steps, I answered your questions by de-
claring, "I am a white, lesbian, feminist, Christian minister doing
her work."

The day you died, a friend called from New York with grief in
her voice. "I have something very sad to tell you, Melanie. Audre's
dead." For years, I had been dreading that news, because I knew
you had been fighting with cancer. I dreaded the day when your
pen would stop touching paper and your earthly body stop touching lives.

In its February 1993 issue, *Sojourner: The Women's Forum* published tributes to you. Kate Rushin remembered the last time she
saw you and that you said to her, "Last week I was dying, but now
I'm not." Rushin also wrote:

> *Precious Audre. We miss her. But there is something we must
> always remember: We, here, are as precious as Audre. Any-
> thing we would hesitate to say to Audre, we best rethink be-*

*fore we say it to each other. Anything we regret not saying to
her, we best say to each other. Anything we wish we had
done for her, we best do for each other.*
  Precious Audre. She was dying, now she's not.
  Precious Audre. You were dying, now you're not.[5]

 In the past few years, I have reclaimed a belief in resurrection as
dangerous memory, as the refusal to forget, the refusal to despair, and
as the subversive, obstinate promise to keep alive the dream of a
world transformed. Elliott, another woman writing in *Sojourner*, put
it this way: "There's a word for loving something we've never
touched: hope."[6]

 Like the resurrected phoenix, hope rose in me from the ashes
of fear when I read your words in *Sister Outsider*. Like a phoenix, you
will keep rising in us every time we speak out and tell the truth
about our lives.

 Thank you, Audre. Thank you.

Melanie

IV

A LOVE THAT
WON'T LET GO

19

In the Presence
of My Enemies

A Communion Meditation

The Psalms express raw human emotion—rage, delight, unmitigated joy, and unguarded pain. In the passionate poetry of the Psalms, accusations of absence and abandonment are hurled at God: "How long, O God, how long? Why have you forsaken me?" And God's presence is pictured in images that are profoundly personal and immediate: "You have been my help, and in the shadow of your wings I sing for joy. My soul clings to you; your right hand upholds me." The Psalms reflect the conviction and expectation that God does not rule the world from some heavenly perch—dispassionate, distant, and removed. Israel's experience is of a God moved by human suffering and oppression. As Moses heard near a desert bush: "I have seen the affliction of my people who are in Egypt. I have heard their cries. I know their sufferings."

In the poetry of the Twenty-third Psalm, we hear the testimony of a person who has experienced God's comforting presence. This presence is described in gestures of divine solicitude and tenderness. The specific circumstances are unknown, but we *do* know that the psalmist is in some kind of danger, living with the threat of death and enemies.

When a passage is as familiar as the Twenty-third Psalm, it is difficult to hear it afresh. A new rendering of the text can help us sit up and take notice:

Although I must enter the darkness of death,
I am not anxious since you are with me—
in your presence I dare to do it.
You invite me to sit at your table,
and all my enemies, with envious eyes,
have to look on while you wait upon me,
while you anoint me, my skin and my hair,
while you fill up my cup to the brim.
Happiness and mercy are coming to meet me
everywhere, every day of my life.[1]

Hearing that translation for the first time, I pictured a scene I had not imagined before in such detail. God invites the psalmist to sit at a table which God lavishly prepares while the psalmist's enemies have to look on with envious eyes. It is a striking image: God attending to this person who has been the object of scorn and the target of violence. The psalmist luxuriates in God's attention, being waited on, given abundant food and drink, and tenderly anointed with soothing oil.

All the while, the assailants, the persecutors, have to watch. They stand there amazed, perplexed, envious, and seemingly help-less. The psalmist, who has been under siege by these enemies, has the deep conviction that they cannot ultimately harm him because God is with him, comforting him, bringing him to an oasis of green, preparing a meal to nurture him, massaging him, and blessing him tenderly.

To grasp the full power of this beautiful image, we need to remember that, in the religious tradition of the psalmist, anointing with oil has rich and varied meanings: oil was used in healing; honored guests were sometimes anointed as a gesture of hospitality; the body of a dead person was anointed with perfumed oils; and ritual anointing was part of the initiation of monarchs, priests, and prophets when they.assumed their office or role. Actually the word "Messiah" or "Christ" literally means: The Anointed One. Anoint-ing with oil, therefore, is a gesture of hospitality, blessing, honor, consecration, and love.[2]

IN THE PRESENCE OF MY ENEMIES   117

The psalmist, who is being threatened with violence and enemies' hatred, pictures God tenderly and joyfully anointing his hair
and skin with oil in an act of blessing and love. In our service today,
we shall follow God's lead by preparing a table and by anointing each
other. Before passing the bread and the cup to one other, you will be
invited to pass a bowl of oil and anoint the person next to you. We
do these things, aware that there are those in this world who have
declared themselves our enemies.

The word "enemy" may sound like an exaggeration; unfortunately, it is not. Recently, I watched a segment of *The 700 Club* in
which Pat Robertson warned of what he calls the "rising storm" of
the gay civil rights movement. He told viewers that the "homosexual lobby," if unchecked, will completely undermine the American
family and everything Americans hold dear. Robertson said that for
a woman to claim that she is proud to be a lesbian is like claiming
that she is proud to be a murderer. He declared that for those
engaged in homosexual behavior, the end will be death and hell, and
that God will punish the United States as Sodom was punished, with
earthquakes and wars.

Similarly, in Lansing, Michigan, a local church is distributing a
brochure that says: "Homosexuality spreads disease rampantly. It kills
and costs billions of dollars for those who are innocent and have
not practiced such lawless deeds." The brochure says that "moral
people" should not be asked to give money to help cure AIDS,
because it is "purely the result of an immoral lifestyle." If "homosex-
uals" would only practice abstinence, "AIDS could be cured in one
generation."

In the last few weeks, a new crisis hotline has been established
in Lansing, sponsored by a group that promises "liberation from
homosexuality." They declare that same-gender sexuality is a sinful
and destructive disorder. This hotline has publicized itself as wanting
to help all kinds of people in all kinds of crises. It was given favorable
coverage in the Lansing daily newspaper.

These are just a few examples of those who have labeled people
with AIDS and gay men and lesbians "enemies." I do not want to
give such people more power than they deserve, but neither do I

want to ignore the threat that they pose. For, in my work as a pastor, I have experienced too many casualties of such hate-filled religious talk that is uttered in the name of God and the Bible.

I am angry and heartbroken when I am called to the bed of a man who is fighting off the ravaging effects of the AIDS virus while also fighting against deeply ingrained religious messages that say he is doomed to eternal suffering. I am angry and grieved that this precious child of God has been robbed of the assurance that he needs: the assurance that he is tenderly loved by a God who would lead him to an oasis of green, where he might stretch out at the edge of the water and find rest.

I am angry and grieved by the number of people I encounter who have been told that their love for another person of the same sex is sin and that their sexual orientation places them outside of God's loving care. I am angry and grieved to experience how deeply that lie can take root in the human spirit, how much work it takes to unearth the lie and plant the seeds of God's love.

I am angry and grieved that in too many churches those of us who are lesbian and gay could not participate in this sacrament of communion or any other aspects of the church's life, unless we remained closeted, invisible, and silent; unless we collaborated with the fear and became, in some sense, our own enemies.

Because of such experiences, some would argue that this sacrament of communion has become meaningless or a symbol of oppression rather than liberation. I beg to differ. We are invited to partake of this communion feast in the spirit of the psalmist, remembering that this feast was prepared for us with love. We are invited to this table while our enemies, with envious eyes, must look on as God waits on us, filling our cup to the brim, tenderly anointing our skin and hair.

As we gather at this welcome table, we come not thumbing our noses at the skeptics or those who call us enemies but remembering how radical it is to sit at this table together, to anoint and bless each other, to believe in the possibility of community that honors differences. We come to the table naming our fears while not allowing them the last word. We come daring to be real about our lives—the pain, the wounds, and the joys. It is a radical act to disavow the lies and to defy the way things are by believing that things can be different. By passing this bread and this cup and by anointing each other with oil, we proclaim a promise for the present and the future. The promise is not that God will magically rescue us from the shadow of death; the promise is that we will be able to walk with one another through that shadow of death when we live, believing that nothing can separate us from the love of God.

INVITATION TO ANOINTING AND COMMUNION

In the presence of our enemies, this table has been lovingly prepared for us. You are invited to take this bowl, dip your fingers in the oil, and anoint your neighbor by making a circle on the palm of her or his hand—a sign of continuity, community, and the love at the heart of the universe. As you anoint your neighbor, say: "Remember that you are loved."

On the night before his death, when the threat of impending violence was palpable, Jesus gathered with his friends to observe the Passover feast. They gathered to celebrate the exodus out of oppression and the long journey toward a promised land. They shared a meal and told the stories of their people, remembering a time when God's liberating presence gave their ancestors courage to resist despair and to journey out and on in hope.

Jesus took the stories and symbols of his faith tradition and reimagined them in a new context. He reimagined the Passover symbols of unleavened bread and wine in the face of enemies who sought to permanently silence his message and his movement. He reimagined the symbols as a way of both naming the threat and recovering hope.

He took the bread, blessed it, gave thanks for it, and said in effect: "As this bread can be broken, they can break my body. They possess the power to do that. But they cannot quench the Spirit or kill the dream of God's creation. Not if you remember. Not if you refuse to forget. Not if you resist being numbed or falling asleep. Every time you eat bread together, remember and keep the dream alive."

And he reimagined the cup by saying in effect: "They may be able to spill my blood, but they can't kill your hope or your experience of forgiving, liberating love. Not if you remember."

Just when we think we are bereft of hope because the powers of death seem to have the upper hand and grief threatens to drown us, our brother Jesus invites us to remember the stories and songs and symbols that inspired our ancestors before us. And he gives us permission to reimagine them in our own context. For here and now, we need courage to remember, to resist despair, and to speak words of hope to each other. So as we pass this bread and this cup, let us say: "Sister, brother, carry on!"

20

G O D W R E S T L I N G

*Again and again in the course of its existence, the Jewish
people has felt itself called by and accountable to a power not
of its own making, a power that seemed to direct its destiny
and give meaning to its life. In both ordinary and extraordin-
ary moments, it has found itself guided by a reality that both
propelled and sustained it and to which gratitude seemed the
only fitting response.*

*The term "Godwrestling" seems appropriate to me to
describe the written residue of these experiences, for I do not
imagine them, a la Cecil B. deMille, as the boomings of a
clear voice or as flashing of tongues of flame, publicly visible,
publicly verifiable, needing only to be transcribed. I imagine
them as moments of profound experience; sometimes of illumination but also of mystery.*[1]

For years, the story of Jacob wrestling in the night has haunted
me. Perhaps it is the struggle and intensity of the story that appeal to
me. Perhaps it is that the meaning of the story is not obvious, not
told to us in some moralistic way—we, too, have to struggle to
understand what is taking place in this nighttime confrontation by a
river between a man named Jacob and some unknown person or
force. Perhaps the story haunts me because it describes faith as a
wrestling in the night.

There is a Dutch painting of people in a church service, seated
serenely, in their finest clothes, looking very proper and almost

bored while in the background Jacob is wrestling for his life. The painting portrays two understandings of faith: first, the conventional, hands folded, obedient, and submissive kind of faith; and second, faith as struggle, wrestling, turmoil. The late Jewish theologian Abraham Heschel once said: "Well-adjusted people think that faith is an answer to all human problems. In truth, however, faith is a challenge to all human answers. Faith is a consuming fire, consuming all pretensions. To have faith is to be in labor."

This life-changing event occurred on the eve of Jacob's confrontation with his brother Esau. Twenty years earlier, Jacob had cheated Esau out of his birthright. Then, pretending to be Esau, Jacob tricked his aging and nearly blind father, Isaac, into blessing him. Suspecting that Esau had neither forgotten nor forgiven him, Jacob sent his wife, children, and companions across the river and stayed behind to spend the night alone. Once before, the night had revealed to Jacob a beautiful vision of a ladder with angels and the promise of God's presence. Perhaps he was hoping for a repeat of that comforting dream. But then, out of the night, came an assailant. . . . "Jacob was left alone and a man wrestled with him until the breaking of the day."

It was a common belief of the time that within the night lived demonic beings with which the legendary hero could do battle and prevail. Perhaps this Jacob story was first told as such a tale. Clearly, Jacob did not know what or who hit him. He fought and wrestled. At first, the unknown combatant seemed malevolent—a nocturnal assailant bent on overwhelming Jacob. Who was this man? a demon? Jacob's shadow side? Jacob's past? Jacob's alter ego? an angel? a divine messenger? God?

And who was holding on to whom? The nameless man overtook Jacob, but as the day began to break, he asked to be released. At this point, Jacob held on, refusing to relinquish his hold until the man blessed him. The encounter is shrouded in the darkness of mystery. We strain to see, but we can only hear the sounds of the struggle by the river's edge.

Although the wrestling had its brutal moments (Jacob's thigh was put out of joint), it also seems to have been a dance of pursuit and retreat. Since it lasted all night, it could not have been brutal as much as clinging, not letting go. The man seems almost to have been playing with Jacob, for he was clearly possessed of greater powers than he used. All he needed to do was "touch" Jacob's thigh to put it out of joint. He did not destroy Jacob, and Jacob began to sense that this assailant had the power to bless him. So then it was Jacob who refused to let go, demanding a blessing.

Where are we at this point, you and I? Are we merely spectators, or do we remember times in our own lives when something completely unexpected took hold of us and refused to let us go? We thought things were under control. At one moment, we were strutting through life, at the next we were fighting to survive. The neat routines, the taken-for-granted occurrences that filled our days, even the fiber of faith that had upheld us and protected us was ripped open. We prayed for God's deliverance but heard only the silence of the night. We fought alone against that which threatened to undo us. Our innocence was ended. We were wounded by the struggle. And we could not remember how it all began. There may have been a precipitating crisis, something that brought us face to face with ourselves. All alone in the night, with defenses gone, we experienced anxiety, depression, fear. At first, we would have done anything to be free of the onslaught: we would have struggled free and run or tried to gain control and put the conflict behind us. But once we had been wounded, nothing could ever be quite the same again. So we scrambled to wrest meaning and a blessing from the encounter. Still seeking to control, we sought assurance.

When Jacob asked for the blessing, the nameless man responded by asking, "What is your name?"—the same question Isaac had asked when Jacob came to him asking for a blessing. When Isaac asked the question, Jacob lied and said, "I am Esau." For the Hebrew people, one's name signified one's identity. Jacob means "One who grasps and supplants." Jacob had come into the world grasping his twin brother's heel; he then had stolen a blessing under false pretenses from his father; and now he was grasping for a new blessing. But this time, he did not lie, he answered, "Jacob." It is unlikely that he felt contrite; nevertheless, he spoke the name and thereby revealed who he was. His past and present were contained in that name.

The man who wrestled with Jacob announced a new name: "Your name will no more be called Jacob, but Israel." Israel means "One who wrestles with God." The community of faith that heard and preserved this story—the people of Israel—confessed, in the telling of this story, their past and present relationship to God. They confessed that they are a people who often struggle with and against God. This name, Israel, expressed a different identity for Jacob. He no longer would be known by his strength alone but also by God's. No longer would his true identity be the one who grasps but rather the one who *is* grasped. It implies a relationship; and, in this relationship with the divine presence, Jacob was neither passive nor in control. As Abraham Heschel said, faith in God is not so much certainty as being in labor, being willing to struggle, wrestle, stay with the process.

Jacob's new name was a gift, but Jacob did not evidence a new character worthy of the gift. He showed neither relinquishment nor gratitude. In fact, he showed more the characteristics of a grasper when he asked, "Tell me, I pray, *your* name."

But the man, knowing Jacob's propensity for grasping and control, asked: "Why is it that you ask my name?" Then, without revealing his name, he blessed Jacob. The sun came up, the man was gone, and Jacob limped away from that place, saying, "I have seen God face to face and yet my life is preserved." What began as something terrifying—a wrestling in the night—had become an experience that Jacob called holy. He emerged from this encounter changed. Although he had been wounded, he had also gained a sense of having wrestled with God.

One of the reasons this story has haunted me for years has to do with my somewhat compulsive drive to wrest meaning from events—my desire to name and thereby think I can control mystery. Perhaps I am haunted by this story because I, like Jacob, trust mostly in my own strength until I am suddenly brought face to face with myself and my flight from God—until I am confronted by someone, something I cannot control. What seems at first to be a threat becomes, in time, a power for transformation and blessing. George MacDonald suggests that God, as a holy and unnamable presence, moves "forward through regions of our darkness into our light";

therefore, long before we are aware of it, God has visited us and is at work. "God may have to begin far back in our spirits, in regions unknown to us, and do much work that we can be aware of only in the results."[2]

MacDonald's description of God's presence illustrates the movement of this story. The encounter moves from the darkness of night to the breaking of day; from what seems to be an assailant to the recognition that Jacob has been visited by God; from the confession of Jacob's past, contained in his name, to the receiving of a new name and a blessing. Jacob, the one who grasped, now has hands laid on him and opens his own hands in a prayer of awe and thanksgiving, beginning to live into his new name.

When we wrestle in resistance, the very embrace of God may be a struggle. The love may be a wound as God will not let us go. But God loves us enough to begin far back in the regions of our darkness, refusing to let go until we are transformed.

The process of healing and transformation, of letting go of an old identity and claiming a new one, can be a terrible struggle. It may feel at times as though it will never end, that the day will never dawn, that the darkness will swallow us up. It can be very difficult to be truthful with ourselves—to name those things that keep us from the deepest source of life and keep us estranged from ourselves and others. In a sense, that is the meaning of the question put to Jacob: "What is your name?" It is a question we all face: "Who are you? What is keeping you from being who you are meant to become?" These are questions that ask us to be truthful. Until we can face and name the truth, we cannot begin to feel the wrestling as an embrace that will bless us and heal us. But like the old Jacob—who prayed before his encounter at the river for deliverance—we may want shortcuts, answers, air-tight certainties. We want to be blessed without having to face who we are. We want a God who will rescue us and do it for us, who will magically solve our dilemmas or problems. We want faith that protects and reassures, rather than faith that is labor and wrestling and real transformation.

I don't mean to make light of the desire for rescue, answers, and release. Enduring the darkness, the wrestling, and the uncertainties can sometimes feel like our demise. It is sometimes impossible to feel we have a shred of faith in God left when the night seems to undo us.

I think of people I know who are in the midst of remembering sexual abuse or incest. They are doing some of the hardest work any human being has to do. For they were, in the past, victims of a different kind of assailant, a perpetrator who then had the power to violate. To survive that violation, they had to shut down and shut out parts of themselves. It is a very different story from Jacob's. But—like Jacob or any of us—in order to heal, to reown those lost parts of themselves, to believe again in their beauty and worth, they must remember. And that remembering takes incredible courage.

I hear people ask, "Where is God? Why must I endure this?" As a pastor, all I can say—if I can say anything at all—is that I do believe that as we walk through the valley of the shadow of death, God will not forsake us. We are God's beloved. God is grieved by the violations done to us, and God holds onto us, not letting us go. I believe God is in the remembering, coming forward through regions of our darkness into our light; and, therefore, long before we are aware of it, God has visited us and is at work.

Blessed are those who dare to be in labor and experience rebirth. Blessed are those who limp from the struggle. Blessed are those who have entered into the darkness of wrestling, not letting go until they receive a blessing and a new name. Blessed are they for they have seen God. And blessed be the name of God forever.

21

IS IT OKAY TO BE
HAPPY?

In junior high and high school, I had a friend named Mary Jo. Being very good friends, we told each other everything we experienced at home, at school, at parties, and on dates (when we had them). Everything. We imitated the voices and gestures of teachers and parents so that no detail of the story would be lost, and especially during these theatrical performances, we laughed ourselves silly.

Mary Jo and I also had serious times. When I stayed overnight at her house and we talked until the wee morning hours, a particular subject would frequently take hold of us. We even had a name for these conversations. We called them "DTs," destiny talks.

In those late-night hours, convinced that every person in the world except the two of us was sound asleep, we considered such questions as: What is life about, anyway? What will be asked of us down the road? Will we have the courage to respond? What or who will we become?

These were deeply spiritual questions, actually—although we seldom spoke in explicitly spiritual terms. Mary Jo and I shared our respective dreams, fantasies, and hunches with each other: about living alone, finding a life partner, or having children; about writing a great novel, getting elected to Congress, living in foreign countries; or about devoting ourselves to some great social cause. Each fantasy was a bit different—sometimes wild, sometimes quite ordinary—but every fantasy was an attempt to articulate our destiny.

It was indeed a serious game we played. We assumed that this thing we called destiny actually existed. It was a given, not entirely ours to create and yet within our power to discover if only we worked hard enough at it. This thought was both compelling and repelling. Just imagine, we said to one another, if we fail to discern our true destiny and pursue the wrong course!

As I remember those conversations, Mary Jo and I had one basic difference in the way we articulated our dreams. She said, "Most of all, I want to be happy. Whatever I do, whoever I am with, I want to be happy." Although I didn't express it aloud to her, I found that sentiment somewhat frivolous. Already in junior high, I had appropriated the belief that happiness isn't something you strive for.

The past couple of years, I have reflected on my skepticism about being happy. In my spiritual world view, meaningful is okay, productive is good, doing something to change the world is *very* good. If, while doing meaningful, productive, socially responsible things, you find a little happiness—more power to you; but happiness should never be a goal. It is a by-product at best, a superficial goal at worst.

I can't simply characterize myself as the product of a Calvinist work ethic. H. L. Mencken once defined a Calvinist as a person who is haunted by the thought that somewhere, someone might be happy. I don't come from a joyless, humorless family that didn't value playfulness. But I did inherit the assumption that if you strive for happiness, you will become materialistic and narcissistic and you will dull the sensitivity to pain that is so essential for growth and true human community. The contempt I learned to feel for the pursuit of happiness is reinforced by clichés like "Don't worry, be happy!" and smiley faces that tell me to "Have a nice day."

I tend to identify things like destiny and spiritual depth with words or phrases like:

> openness to change
> struggle
> wrestling
> being in labor
> ferment
> sensitivity to suffering

compassion
solidarity

Not a lot of happiness in that list! I've come to see that it is I who make happiness frivolous by not giving it sufficient room in my life. As a person whose spirituality has been much more activist than contemplative, I don't need to be told: Don't just stand there, in God's name, do something! I need to hear: Don't just do something, in God's name, stand there![1]

The psalmist said it this way: "Be still and know that I am God." Lao Tsu put it another way: "Practice non-action. Work without doing. Magnify the small, increase the few. See simplicity in the complicated."[2] And Jesus said: "Look at the birds of the air; they neither sow nor reap nor gather into barns, and yet God your heavenly Father and Mother feeds them. . . . Consider the lilies of the field, how they grow; they neither toil nor spin, yet I tell you, even Solomon in all his glory was not arrayed like one of these."[3]

Yet another objection surfaces within me: Is it okay to be happy when a brother or sister is in pain and when there is so much unhappiness all around, so much violence, so much suffering?

One of the people who has been a teacher for me when I ask such questions is Etty Hillesum, the Jewish author who died in Auschwitz at the age of twenty-nine.[4] Etty believed that our human vocation, our spiritual calling, is to safeguard that little piece of God that is found in each of us—to make a safe dwelling place for God to be at home in this world. She believed our vocation is to help God, not the other way around. And she believed that no pain or joy ought to be discounted as too small. By listening to and deeply feeling every pain, every joy, Etty explains, we are not self-indulgent in some unspiritual way. Quite the contrary: by attending to every pain and joy, we come closer to God who is within each of us.[5]

I find it so moving that just before Etty's train pulled into Auschwitz, she flung from the window a postcard that was later discovered by a farmer. On it she had scribbled: "We have entered the camp singing." She knew what lay ahead. It was not denial that had her singing. It was her resistant, victoriously joyful self that refused to let her humanity be crushed. For her to have done otherwise would have allowed the enemy to truly win. I am likewise moved by her prayer, written during a bleak winter of German occupation and persecution:

> *The jasmine behind my house has been completely ruined by the rains and storms of the last few days, its white blossoms are floating about in muddy black pools on the low garage roof. But somewhere inside me the jasmine continues to blossom undisturbed, just as profusely and delicately as ever it did. And it spreads its scent round the House in which You dwell, oh God. You can see, I look after You, I bring You not only my tears and my forebodings on this stormy, grey Sunday morning. I even bring You scented jasmine. And I shall bring You all the flowers I shall meet on my way, and truly there are many of those. I shall try to make You at home always. Even if I should be locked up in a narrow cell and a cloud should drift past my small barred window, then I shall bring You that cloud, oh God, while there is still the strength in me to do so.[6]*

Etty Hillesum is one of the those teachers, like Jesus and Lao Tsu, who remind me at what cost I do the splittings, saying that feeling deep pain means I ought not to feel deep joy or that being happy will somehow be a barrier to recognizing injustice. Those are false splittings. Can my fretting add a single hour to my lifespan? Can my long face really do anything to reduce another's pain?

My Dutch friend Riet told me how her four-year-old grandson Pieter loves to climb on her lap and snuggle with her. Recently, he asked Riet: "Grandma, do you know what is the bestest thing in the whole world that people can do?"

"What Pieter?" asked Riet.

Putting his cheek next to hers and rubbing softly, Pieter replied, "Skin on skin!"

Taking a child from his lap and putting the child into the middle of a circle of adults, Jesus announced that unless his hearers became like that child, they would not be able to experience the Spirit's gifts of abundant life and the commonwealth of God.

Before it was shamed out of us, we naturally had the capacity to feel pain as pain, injustice as injustice, happiness as happiness. You know the sheer wonder that can overcome a child who is observing something beautiful—a magic stone, the veins of a leaf, or the music of a warbling bird. Little Nathan who lives down the street from me cannot talk yet, but when I take his hand and we go for a walk, he is constantly pointing to things. He wants me to see. And he turns to me beaming. Even when it is the fourteenth squirrel he has seen that day, he is grinning at the sheer wonder of it all.

One of the challenges of being, and staying human, is to take life seriously without taking ourselves too seriously. As Emma Goldman said so many years ago: "If I can't dance, I don't want to be a part of your revolution." If there is no room for dancing, for singing, for laughter and celebration in the midst of all our work and efforts and struggle, then we become grim and joyless. If we no longer can be surprised by joy, it is a clear indication that even our best intentions and good causes have gone sour. Joy and happiness aren't things we can plan, calculate, organize, create, or demand. They can only be received and savored or passed by and lost—like the intense happiness of being fully alive, of seeing a friend's face, of sensing a deep connectedness with earth and sky and water, of forgiving and being forgiven, or the delight of skin on skin.

Through the ages, the commonwealth of God has been pictured as a feast, with much dancing and singing and joy. Communion is, among other things, a celebration of that commonwealth time when barriers will be removed and all people will eat together at the table of life.

Some years ago while living in the Netherlands, I had an experience of communion I shall never forget. I had been asked by Piet and Gelda to perform their wedding. Piet worked at Rainbow House, a group home for teenagers and young adults with developmental disabilities. Piet and Gelda had invited the residents of Rainbow House to the wedding; and, at the couple's request, we planned to celebrate communion as part of the ceremony. But shortly before the wedding, we learned that some of the parents of the young people with whom Piet worked did not want their children to participate in the communion service because they had never become formal members of their church. Membership involved being able to recite the Heidelberg Catechism; and, in their church, unless you were a member, you couldn't receive communion.

When we heard this, we decided to scrap the idea of communion; it was unacceptable to us for these young people to have to remain seated and watch while the rest of us came forward for communion. It felt like a complete contradiction of the meaning of celebrating communion. However, at the last minute, the parents relented and granted their permission for this special occasion.

One by one, members of the congregation came forward—friends and family of Piet and Gelda. Most of the people received the bread and cup with a serious expression, taking the bread and nodding silently—something they had done many times.

Then the residents of Rainbow House came forward. Their faces were beaming. When I offered them the bread, they exclaimed loudly and gestured: "Oooh, aaaah. . . ." Some of them took the bread and held it, examining it from different angles, smelling it, fingering it, putting it tenderly to their lips and tongue before eating it.

As they returned to their seats, they ran to Piet and Gelda and covered them with hugs and kisses, making a terrible, wonderful racket in the otherwise silent sanctuary. And I knew I had, at last, experienced what a communion service is supposed to be: a love feast, a passionate, sensual celebration of what the African American gospel song calls "that happy day."

22

REFRAINING FROM EXPLAINING

I met Anne several years ago at a conference. As we talked, she confided in me that she was very angry with God. Anne was an only child, and when she was eight years old both of her parents had been killed in an auto accident. She was old enough to understand what the minister said at her parent's funeral: "The Lord gives and the Lord takes away. God's ways are not our ways. Difficult as it is to understand and accept, God must have had a purpose in taking these two people to himself." In Anne's presence, this minister declared that the death of her parents had been the will of God. Why this minister said this I can't tell you. Perhaps he thought such words would be comforting. Maybe he thought as a minister he had to be able to "explain" and give theological reasons for such a tragedy. I don't know; but at the most terrifying, most vulnerable, moment of her life she heard that God is a God who wanted her parents to die.

Is it any wonder that Anne grew up seeing God as her enemy, as someone to fear? Anne told me that from that moment on she had been afraid to love anyone, for she secretly believed that God would one day also take that loved one away from her. As Anne grew older, fear was replaced by anger at God. "Why had God let such a thing happen?" she asked.

Pauline and Carl Green were members of a congregation I served. Five years before I came to the church, the Green's six-year-old grandchild had drowned in a neighbor's swimming pool. Five years later, some of the things that people said to them at the time of the funeral, in an effort to extend comfort, were still fresh in their minds: "God took your grandchild because He wanted a little angel by His side." Others said: "Maybe God wanted to spare your grandson all the pain that can come with growing older."

Why do people such as Anne's minister and the friends of the Greens say such things? One reason may be that they have uncritically accepted certain images of God as omnipotent—meaning almighty and all powerful. And they think that believing in God means believing that whatever happens—however terrible—is somehow "caused" by God. So they say such things, as it were, to defend God.

Or maybe they need to defend themselves, protect themselves against pain. They feel powerless and think they have to come up with something comforting. Not knowing how to just sit with another person, hold that person, and weep with that person, they offer what they think are comforting words by trying to make sense of the senseless.

These are rather dramatic examples of affixing God's name to events. We may do this same kind of thing, however, in smaller ways. Almost twenty years ago, I lived with some friends named Brad and Margaret. We would laugh together about Margaret's tendency to assume that God was "teaching her a lesson." Once Margaret was irritated with some annoying habit of mine; but, rather than tell me about it, she let her anger fester. Then one night, I missed the subway and didn't come home when I was expected. When I finally walked in three hours late, Margaret hugged me and expressed great relief: "I was so afraid you were lying in some ditch somewhere and God was teaching me a lesson, showing me that I shouldn't be angry with you about stupid things."

I responded: "Great! I get sacrificed so that you can learn a lesson! Wouldn't there be a better way to teach you the lesson? A way that would prove a bit fairer to me?"

All of these stories illustrate our tendency to name, and thereby misname, events we cannot understand by attributing some divine cause to them. Most likely, none of these people—not the minister in Anne's story, the people who said those things to the Greens, or Margaret in her moment of guilty fretting—really grasped what they were saying about who God is: a being or force or spirit who wills a tragic accident that leaves an eight-year-old child alone in the world or who likes to take little children away from parents and grandparents or who teaches some people lessons by harming others. If we were to listen more carefully to what we say, we might at least hesitate before defining an event as God's will or saying things like: "I guess it was meant to be."

There are times when it would be best for us to refrain from affixing God's name or karma or any other cosmic or divine cause to experiences. I can feel tremendous anger when I think of Anne's minister saying with such authority that God willed that terrible accident. He took the name of God in vain. I can feel as much anger when my friend in the Netherlands, after several years of unsuccessful attempts to become pregnant, is told by friends that "a baby has not yet chosen her." Or when victims of sexual abuse are told that this experience of assault *had* to happen in order for them to work out some piece of unfinished karma from another life.

If we cannot share in the grief that another person is experiencing, we at least can refrain from trying to explain it away. I personally don't know about babies' spirits seeking out mothers' bodies to be born into or about unfinished karma—those are things I have neither studied nor worked at understanding. What I *do* know is that the God I believe in does not will suffering.

Part of the confusion stems from our tendency to think in mutually exclusive absolutes. We say that "there is no such thing as an accident," or we say that "everything is random and accidental." Neither statement reflects my deepest experience or belief.

I believe that there is a creative purpose at the heart of the universe; a source or power that is *for* us, not *against* us. And that power or source, which I call "God," wills or longs for us to be restored to this state of love, reconciliation, justice, and peace.

The God revealed in the words, actions, stories, and life of Jesus from Nazareth is a God who yearns for our healing, wholeness, and liberation but never robs us of our freedom. We are free to choose life or to choose against it; to choose love or against it; we can do life-giving things or self-destructive things. The God that Jesus speaks of is a God who suffers with us as we suffer. A God of exodus and resurrection. A God whose name is "I Am Who I Am, I

Will Be There for You." A God who gave Moses the strength to say to Pharaoh: "Let my people go!"

To say that God wills or longs that I discover and act in accordance with this way of love and justice is different from saying that God has mapped out every little episode of my life. To say that I may have unique ways of being a channel of God's loving presence is different from saying that God has a detailed plan of my every step. To say that in every circumstance—even the hardest, most trying circumstances—I might still know God's loving presence, does not mean that God has willed or ordained every circumstance that befalls me.

There have been times when I glimpsed the meaning of my existence. There have been moments when I have been overcome with the sheer beauty of creation or the gift of being known and loved and accepted for who I am. Illumination has also occurred in times of great distress and grief. In such moments, it is as if the curtain is torn away, I see into the heart of things and sigh, "Aha! Yes! Yes! This is what it is all about."

I cannot manufacture such moments—they are beyond my power or control. I feel I am standing in the presence of mystery. I want, as it were, to remove my shoes. This ground, that just a moment ago was ordinary, now feels like holy ground. And I sense at such moments that life is not just a series of random occurrences without meaning, without purpose. I sense at such moments that there is something more eternal than chaos, something more lasting than death, something stronger than evil.

Those rare moments of breakthrough, illumination, and grace feel like moments of convergence. You could call them "burning bush" experiences. It feels as if I were meant to be standing in this place at this moment or to be undergoing this event at this time. Surely, this can't be an accident!

But sometimes I wonder: Was only *that* bush at *that* place in the desert at *that* moment in Moses' life alive with God's presence and purpose? Or was Moses, because of all that led up to that moment, finally able to recognize, hear, and respond to something, someone, who had been calling his name all along? Perhaps every bush is potentially a burning bush. I think of the line from George Bernard

Shaw's *Joan of Arc,* in which King Charles asks Joan why she thinks she is special in being able to hear God's voice in the chiming of cathedral bells: "Why don't the voices come to me? I am king, not you!" Joan replies: "They do come to you; but you do not hear them. You have not sat in the field in the evening listening for them. . . . if you prayed from your heart, and listened to the thrilling of the bells in the air after they stop ringing, you would hear the voices as well as I do."[1]

To say that life is not merely a series of random accidents is not to deny that accidents happen—because they do happen. I don't believe, as some might, that every person in an airplane crash has met his or her appointed hour. I don't believe that each of us has some date of death—what people call "our time to go"—that is destined by the stars or written in a heavenly calendar. Such a belief profoundly contradicts what I believe about human freedom and choice.

Accidents happen, and terrible, undeserved things happen to innocent people. Are we to believe, as some might want us to, that God is smiling more favorably on the United States at this moment than on famine-stricken Somalia? that those innocent children somehow deserve their hunger or are learning some lesson from it? The crisis in Somalia is clearly no accident, but not because God willed it. There are human causes for the suffering, just as there are human solutions to it. To respond with justice and compassion to the situation may be to respond to God's will.

Sometimes people who are in the midst of suffering due to illness, imprisonment, or injustice experience God's presence and a sense of deep meaning. Suffering can also be the context in which the curtain is torn and we see into the heart of things. Sometimes we hear people say things like: "I feel almost grateful for my cancer, because maybe if I had been healthy I would not have been forced to look at my life with such clarity. Maybe I would not have come to understand and believe what I now believe."

Again, let us take care. To say that we can experience God's presence, God's love, God's purpose as we face cancer or other life-threatening circumstances is very different from saying that God gave us (or another person) cancer so that we might learn from it.

The psalmist says: "Even though I walk through the valley of the shadow of death, I fear no evil for you are with me, and your presence comforts me." To say that God is present with those who suffer is very different from saying that God *wills* suffering. To say that God's Spirit can be called upon to sustain us in times of anguish and grief is very different from saying that God desires for us to undergo such times.

Terrible things happen, and God's name is attributed to them—war, violence, torture. God is also blamed for not intervening and stopping such things. I believe that God works in this world to stop such things through you and me, through human beings like Moses who resist the oppressors. God has no other hands than ours. God needs us to say "yes" to life and "no" to death in all its forms.

There are other occurrences for which we can find no explanation: terrible things happen to some people and not to others; some people live into their nineties while others die in childhood. We would do well, I believe, to refrain from affixing God's name to such things. We must recognize that there are things we do not and cannot understand.

In the presence of mysteries—those that fill us with awe and those that fill us with horror—perhaps the best we can do is to remove our shoes. Remove them as an act of reverence when we sense we are on holy ground. Remove them as an act of respect so as not to trample on others with our explanations. Perhaps the best we can say is that we do not know why some things happen or why life is sometimes so unfair. But we *do* know the name of the One who promises not to forsake us: I Am Who I Am, I Will Be There for You.

23

TELLING THE TRUTH
ABOUT OUR LIVES

For too many years, I tried to live out my ministry in the church without acknowledging my identity as a lesbian. Until the duplicity grew so thick it threatened to choke me. Until I realized that I had lost my voice and was in danger of losing any sense of integrity.

Now that I am out of the church's closet, I find myself tempted to hide in a new one. As I become more involved in working with other lesbians to advocate change, I am hesitant to acknowledge my identity as a Christian. Many lesbians that I respect have left the church, having experienced double jeopardy at the hands of an institution that has often proclaimed bad news rather than good for women in general and for lesbian women in particular.

I find that my ordination can be an initial barrier as these women meet me, and I am frequently asked how I can possibly remain identified with Christianity. Being a minority within a minority has pushed me to articulate why Christianity continues to engage me. I share many of the questions my post-Christian lesbian sisters raise about the Christian tradition and ask myself: What is it in this tradition that is liberating and life giving for me, and what can I not find elsewhere, outside the church?

The first thing I name out loud when pressed to "give account for the hope that is within me" is confession. If I were no longer part of a worshiping community, I would miss many aspects of worship. But most of all, I would miss the invitation to confession and the announcement of forgiveness. Nowhere else am I weekly confronted with this discipline of honestly acknowledging individual and collective complicity in the sin I daily encounter. Nowhere else am I confronted with the promise that I am free and the reminder that I am obliged to begin anew.

The liturgical practice of confession is different from the personal discipline of being scrupulous and honest with oneself. Confession in the midst of a community opens doors into myself that self-denial had kept locked. When I hear another person put her confession into words, it can startle me into new, initially painful, self-revelation. As Adrienne Rich says, "When someone tells me a piece of the truth which has been withheld from me, and which I needed in order to see my life more clearly, it may bring acute pain, but it can also flood me with a cold, sea-sharp wash of relief.[1]

When I say that I have not found any other place or context where I am called to tell the truth about my life and to hear the promise of forgiveness, I mean that I have found no place except the church where both things are set before me simultaneously—and one without the other can become either oppressive or trivial. Confession without the promise of forgiveness is ultimately unbearable; forgiveness without the discipline of confession is cheap grace.

In the lesbian community (sometimes more frequently than in the church), I have encountered people who are willing to be very confessional, although they might not call it that. I have found women who are willing to examine the ways that they (we) participate in maintaining racism, ableism, classism, and other systemic forms of oppression. I have witnessed honest dialogue and painstaking efforts to eliminate these systemic sins in the lesbian community. When we fail, however, as we inevitably do, and are brought face to face with once again having been guilty of perpetuating racism, for example, I have longed for us to be able to speak a word of self-forgiveness aloud. Without forgiveness, the weight of complicity can drive us into despair or self-righteousness.

On the other hand, there are places or contexts where I have heard forgiveness proclaimed in a way that bypasses the hard work of truth telling. There is, for example, a misuse of some contemporary therapeutic concepts that would have us believe that all shame is dysfunctional. The capacity to feel shame for behavior that has been harmful is a sign of our humanity.

During the Gulf War, I needed a community of people with whom I could confess my shame as a United States citizen; a community in which I could truthfully acknowledge that bodies and not only buildings were being ripped apart; a community of people with whom I could weep. I needed a confessing community.

That need is ongoing, because as Adrienne Rich says, "Truthfulness, honor, is not something which springs ablaze of itself; it has to be created between people."[2] Although Adrienne Rich was not writing about liturgical confession in these words about truthfulness, they express what I experience when, as a congregation, we are invited to tell the truth about our lives. Rich is not romantic about the process of truth telling. She names it "delicate . . . often terrifying" to the persons involved.[3] Yet she affirms the process of truth telling for the same reasons I affirm that I need a confessing and forgiving community:

> It is important to do this because it breaks down human self-delusion and isolation.
>
> It is important to do this because in so doing we do justice to our own complexity.
>
> It is important to do this because we can count on so few people to go that hard way with us.[4]

24

THE PEARL OF

GREAT PRICE

I was attending one of my first social events in the lesbian community in Lansing, some years ago. After we had consumed the potluck dinner, our host called us together for introductions, suggesting we go around the group, saying our names and telling something about our work and other activities. My heart started pounding—not because such group introductions normally frighten me, but because I didn't want to announce to a group of lesbians that I am a minister.

When my turn came, I talked instead about the antihomophobia and feminism workshops I was leading. But when I yielded the floor to the next person, the woman on my other side (who knew me slightly) elbowed me and whispered in a voice audible to the whole group, "Tell them you're a Christian minister!" Red-faced and caught, I mumbled something about being a minister.

After the introductions, I was cornered by a woman who demanded to know how I, as a self-respecting lesbian, could have anything to do with Christianity, given that it was thoroughly patriarchal and misogynist. I told her that I would answer her if she truly wanted to know and expressed my concern that she had already decided my beliefs could not have integrity. She claimed she wanted to know, although she never really lost her aggressive edge. As I explained to her which parts of the tradition I embraced and which parts I disowned, I realized that a small circle had gathered and was listening to our conversation. I noticed one woman in particular who listened intently.

Several months later, I got a phone call from the woman who

had listened but said nothing. She explained that she had met me at a dinner and was calling now because she was seriously, probably terminally, ill and needed to talk with someone who took spiritual questions seriously. When we met to talk further, I felt intense gratitude for that woman who had elbowed me into self-identification as a Christian minister. Both she and the woman who had accosted me had called me to give account for the hope that is within me and that accounting spurred this sacred meeting.

Coming out as a Christian within the lesbian community has meant, on more than one occasion, that I have been challenged to give account of the pearl of hope that I still find in the field of Christianity. I have only found this pearl by digging deep, below the surface platitudes and billboard announcements that "Jesus is the answer"; below the creeds that have attempted to capture and encapsulate the pearl in their rigid doctrines and definitions; below the patriarchal dualisms that have made a hierarchy of man over woman, spirit over body, heaven over earth.

I am convinced that if I were to dig deep enough, my hands would touch the hands of people who began in other fields, in other spiritual traditions. I believe that deep, deep down, spiritual truth is one. There are many paths, many fields, but truth is indivisible. That is why when I have encountered wise people of spiritual traditions different from mine—Native American, Jewish, Hindu, Buddhist—they do not encourage me to forsake the Christian field in which I am rooted but to dig deeper. They don't encourage me to appropriate their traditions but to seek the wisdom at the heart of my own.

While digging in the field where I am growing, I need to be in conversation with those digging in other fields. Without appropriating or stealing, Christians need the spiritual gifts and wisdom gleaned from other spiritual traditions. I believe that Christianity, by itself, cannot bring us into right relationship with the earth.[1] For that pressing spiritual challenge, we need the wisdom of other spiritual paths. I am also convinced that Christianity, by itself, cannot bring me into right relationship with my lesbian sensuality/sexuality. For that, I need the spiritual wisdom of mentors and sisters such as Audre Lorde, Adrienne Rich, and Marilyn Frye.

Nevertheless, there is a pearl of great price that we lesbian and gay Christians have found as we dig with our lives, our questions, our rage, our grief, our survival, our hope, our experience of being told by the church that we were unworthy because of who we are and who we love. It is a pearl buried in the field of Christianity, buried beneath the church that tried to exclude us and condemn us. That pearl is the conviction that nothing, absolutely nothing, can separate us from the love of God—not closets, threats of violence, self-hatred, shame, bigotry, or the weapon of fear.

When I hold that pearl in my hands and let its power really sink in, then I understand Jesus' parable of the treasure hidden in a field and the wild abandon and joy of the person who discovers the treasure. When I live from the conviction that nothing can separate me from the love of God, then I do not fear what my enemies fear nor am I intimidated by them.

Contained within this pearl is yet another: that love and justice are inseparable. The scriptures witness to the fact that justice, every bit as much as love, reveals the heart of God. Love without justice is sentimental and naive; justice without love can be harsh and unmerciful. The promise of unconditional love is not that God will bless unconditionally all that we are or do. The promise is that even when we are judged and found wanting, love never ends.

Remembering that love is only love when it is rooted in justice reminds us that "sin" and "redemption" are corporate as well as individual realities. Sin is, as Carter Heyward says, "our denial or violation of right relation, our rejection of movement toward mutuality."[2] Redemption is restoration of right relation and mutuality. Individuals may participate in the denial and violation of right relation, but sin is also manifest in systems of oppression. Therefore, the work of redemption requires that we seek to change systems and not only individuals.

Recognizing the inseparability of love and justice means cultivating a commitment to resist oppression in all its forms. It can be liberating to hear that nothing can separate us from the love of God and to know that those who would silence and oppress lesbians and gay men will not have the last word. Such liberating love does not, however, make lesbians and gay men immune to oppressing others. Those of us who are white and lesbian or gay participate daily in racist systems of oppression. It is, therefore, not enough to create church communities that welcome lesbians and gay men if other systemic forms of evil are ignored.

It is a wonderful thing to be able to say "I am lesbian, I am gay, and I am proud." But the pearl of great price is a pearl of love rooted in justice for *all*. When we hold this pearl in our hands we are compelled to adopt a vigilant spirit that respects the worth and pride of *every* person and that seeks to recognize, confess, and change the ways we benefit from power over others. As long as systemic injustice exists in forms such as anti-Semitism, racism, sexism, and heterosexism, our churches cannot be "safe" spaces. If we strive for safety, we may cover over differences among us and circumvent the hard work required of us. Love that is rooted in justice does not aim for peace at all costs—its aim is transformation. So long as systemic injustice exists, transformation will involve not only changes in attitudes or behaviors, but also fundamental redistribution of power.[3] Holding the pearl of great price in our hands, we can do no less than commit ourselves to the goal of transformation. Unless we have hold of that pearl, we may not be able to sustain such hard work.

It is a good discipline to be called to account for the hope that is within us. In honor of every woman or man who has cornered me and called me to such an accounting, I offer this:

I believe there is a just and loving Spirit at the heart of the universe that yearns for each of us to be healed, to find our power, and to know we are loved. Nothing we do can destroy this holy connection with us, although we may choose to hide from it or deny it.

I believe this Spirit is outraged and suffers with every act of violence, abuse of power, or widening of alienation. She will not coerce, control, or manipulate. She travels with us as ally, advocate, survival strength, persistence, and creativity in the struggle for justice.

I believe that life, death, and resurrection are realities facing me every day.

I do *not* believe there is some grand design or plan for my life determined by the rotation of planets, karma, or an Almighty Father God.

I believe, instead, in the terrifying possibility and responsibility of being free to choose between life and death in big and small ways. I believe I am accountable for my choices. I believe it matters what I choose.

I believe it is a holy and human task to work to minimize injustice and to resist death in all its forms—such as sexism, racism, and heterosexism. It is also a holy and human task to nurture connections, justice, reconciliation, and love.

I believe that human beings are capable of attaining great heights and creating great horrors. I believe that the greatest damage is done when we deny our own capacity for doing violence; when we project what we fear in ourselves onto others, name them enemy, and seek to destroy them. I therefore need the ritual and community practice of confession which invites me to name my own woundedness, broken-heartedness, and complicity—not for the sake of feeling guilty but for the sake of experiencing forgiveness and finding new courage.

I believe that the Spirit of just love will not haunt me with my wrong choices, my failure of nerve, my silence, or my concessions to fear. She will invite me again and again to move with her, to open further, and to dare more. If I will let her, She will go with me into unfamiliar places, further than I could ever imagine. She will even help me glimpse the human face of my enemies and the shadow side of myself.

I am haunted by Jesus—the man, the Jew, the guide, the teacher, the visionary, the lover, the passionate one, the anointed one. He is for me a messianic figure in the sense that his life, deeds, and words point me toward a way of being and a realm of being in which the world will be restored to its original meaning and purpose: a peaceable commonwealth, the reign of God.

I don't know what it means to say, "I believe in Jesus," but I do know that I believe Jesus when he speaks of God. I find him believable, trustworthy, and compelling when he speaks about who God is and who we can be as human beings.[4]

I believe Jesus wants me to know that I can have an intimate relationship with God, as intimate—in my own way—as his was. I also believe that I must do my own living and dying, believing and choosing; Jesus won't do those things for me.

My people, my community of faith, are those in every time, place, spiritual tradition, and tongue:

> who live passionately,
> who are animated by God's dream for creation,
> who do not give up hope or the struggle (even against great odds and much defeat),
> who feel deeply,
> who are capable of grief as well as humor,
> and who seek to reconstitute the world.[5]

I believe, with Martin Luther King Jr., that unarmed truth and unconditional love will have the final word.[6] I believe that nothing, absolutely nothing, can separate us from the love of God. That is the pearl of great price that has been unearthed for me by digging with my sisters and brothers in the field called Christianity.

NOTES

INTRODUCTION

1. The literal meaning of the word "conspire" is "to breathe together." Coconspirators are those who breathe with one another.

1. STANDING ON HOLY GROUND

1. Louis I. Newman, *The Hasidic Anthology: Tales and Teachings of the Hasidim* (New York: Charles Scribner's Sons, 1934), 221.

3. SINGING HOPE'S SONG IN A STRANGE LAND

1. Adrienne Rich, "Sources," in *Your Native Land, Your Life* (New York: W. W. Norton and Company, 1986), 25, 27.

4. THE HEART OF THE MATTER

1. Marilyn Frye, *The Politics of Reality: Essays in Feminist Theory* (Trumansburg, N.Y.: The Crossing Press, 1983), 148.
2. Anthropologist Mary Douglas makes a compelling case for understanding holiness as wholeness and completion in *Purity and Danger: An Analysis of the Concepts of Pollution and Taboo* (London: Routledge, 1966), 42–58.

3. Ibid., 54.

4. For this definition of sin, I am indebted to Larry Rasmussen's comment in unpublished lectures on "Jesus and Power." According to Rasmussen, Jesus saw "the essence of sin as the exclusion of some from the ranks of the rest."

5. James Nelson, "Relationships: Blessed and Blessing" (presented at the Twelfth Annual National Gathering of the United Church Coalition for Lesbian and Gay Concerns, St. Paul, Minn., June 26, 1992), 2.

5. YOU ARE MY BELOVED

1. Bonnie Angelo, "The Pain of Being Black," *Time*, 22 May 1989, 120.

2. Susan Bowers, "*Beloved* and the New Apocalypse," *Journal of Ethnic Studies* 18, no. 1 (spring 1990): 66.

3. Ibid., 74.

4. Toni Morrison, *Beloved* (New York: Alfred A. Knopf, 1987), 261.

5. Ibid., 272–73.

6. Lawrence Kushner, *Honey from the Rock: Visions of Jewish Mystical Renewal* (San Francisco: Harper and Row, 1977), 60.

6. CREATING NEW RITUALS: RITES OF PASSAGE IN LESBIAN AND GAY COMMUNITIES

1. John Boswell, *Christianity, Social Tolerance, and Homosexuality: Gay People in Western Europe from the Beginning of the Christian Era to the Fourteenth Century* (Chicago: University of Chicago Press, 1980), 15.

2. Ibid., 16.

3. Ibid., 16–17.

4. Frye, 148–49.

5. Ibid., 149–50.

6. Carter Heyward, *Touching Our Strength: The Erotic as Power and the Love of God* (San Francisco: Harper and Row, 1989), 3.

7. This declaration of commitment was inspired by and adapted from a pronouncement written by Linda Hansen and quoted in Becky Butler, ed., *Ceremonies of the Heart: Celebrating Lesbian Unions* (Seattle: Seal Press, 1990), 198.

7. THE POWER OF SAYING GOD-SHE

1. Rita M. Gross, "Female God Language in a Jewish Context," in *Womanspirit Rising: A Feminist Reader in Religion*, ed. Carol P. Christ and Judith Plaskow (San Francisco: Harper and Row, 1979), 167–73.

2. Carter Heyward, *Our Passion for Justice* (New York: The Pilgrim Press, 1984), 25.

8. GOOD SHAME/BAD SHAME

1. Gershen Kaufman, *Shame: The Power of Caring* (Rochester, Vt.: Schenkman Books, 1980), 8.

2. Ibid., 8.

3. Ibid., 9.

4. Ibid., 11–15.

5. Ibid., 71–84.

6. Ibid., 91–94.

7. Robert Terry, "The Negative Impact on White Values," in *Impacts of Racism on White Americans*, ed. Benjamin P. Browser and Raymond Hunt (Newbury Park, Calif.: Sage Publications, 1981), 120.

8. Joseph Barndt, *Dismantling Racism: The Continuing Challenge to White America* (Minneapolis: Augsburg, 1991), 55.

9. Adrienne Rich quotes these words by Julia de Burgos in her poem, "North American Time," in *Your Native Land, Your Life*, 36. In a note, Rich identifies her source as "Julia de Burgos (1914–1953), Puerto Rican poet and revolutionary who died on the streets of New York City."

10. John P. Fernandez with Mary Barr, *The Diversity Advantage* (New York: Lexington Books, 1993), 247.

11. Donna K. Bivens and Nancy D. Richardson, "Naming and Claiming Our Histories," *The Brown Papers* 1, no. 2 (Nov. 1994), 13. Copies of *The Brown Papers* can be ordered from the Women's Theological Center, P.O. Box 1200, Boston, MA 02117-1200.

12. Ibid., 12.

9. HUMILITY RECONSIDERED

1. Alice Walker, *The Color Purple* (New York: Washington Square Press, 1982), 178.

11. IN THIS *KAIROS* MOMENT

1. Nelle Morton, *The Journey Is Home* (Boston: Beacon Press, 1985), 75.
2. Ibid., 76.
3. Katie G. Cannon, Beverly W. Harrison, Carter Heyward, Ada Maria Isasi-Diaz, Bess B. Johnson, Mary D. Pellauer, and Nancy D. Richardson, *God's Fierce Whimsy: Christian Feminism and Theological Education* (New York: The Pilgrim Press, 1985), 134.
4. Gross, 167–73.
5. Heyward, *Our Passion for Justice,* 27.

13. RISING LIKE THE PHOENIX:
A NEW CHURCH MOVEMENT

1. I am indebted to John Linsheid for the discovery of these verses in Isaiah (56:1–8) and recommend his interpretation of this and other biblical passages in "Our Story in God's Story: How I Began Reading the Bible through Gay Eyes," in *Christians and Homosexuality: Dancing toward the Light,* 1994, a special issue booklet available from *The Other Side,* 300 W. Apsley, Philadelphia, PA 19144.

15. REMEMBERING RE-IMAGINING

1. These words are quoted from the statement of welcome in the Re-Imagining Conference program book given to registered participants, 2.
2. "Bishop Hunt Addresses Sophia," *Good News* (March/April 1994): 17.
3. The words and music of the song we sang that day were written by Pat Humphries. The song is titled, "Never Turning Back." Copyright © 1984 Pat Humphries. Moving Forward Music.

18. LETTER TO AUDRE

1. Margaret Randall, in "A Tribute to Audre Lorde," *Sojourner: The Women's Forum* (Feb. 1993): 14.
2. Audre Lorde, *Sister Outsider* (Trumansburg, N.Y.: Crossing Press, 1984), 41.
3. Ibid., 42.

4. Ibid., 44.
5. Kate Rushin, "Tribute," 12.
6. Elliott, "Tribute," 16.

19. IN THE PRESENCE OF MY ENEMIES

1. Huub Oosterhuis, Michel van der Plas, Pius Drijvers, Han Renckens, Frans Jozef van Beeck, David Smith, and Forrest Ingram, *Fifty Psalms: An Attempt at a New Translation* (London: Burns and Oates; New York: Herder and Herder, 1969), 36.
2. Madeleine S. Miller and J. Lane Miller, *The Harper's Bible Dictionary* (New York: Harper and Brothers, 1959), 20.

20. GODWRESTLING

1. Judith Plaskow, *Standing Again at Sinai: Judaism from a Feminist Perspective* (San Francisco: Harper and Row, 1990), 33.
2. C. S. Lewis, *George MacDonald Anthology* (London: Geoffrey Bles, 1946), 56.

21. IS IT OKAY TO BE HAPPY?

1. I do not know the exact origin of this play on words. Years ago, I had a poster with Daniel Berrigan's portrait on it, along with the words: "Don't just do something, stand there!" Perhaps it was a quote from Berrigan, but I can't be sure.
2. Lao Tsu, "Saying Number Sixty-three," in *Tao Te Ching: A New Translation*, trans. Gia-Fu Feng and Jane English (New York: Vintage Books, 1972).
3. Matt. 6:26, 28–29, in *The Gospels and the Letters of Paul: An Inclusive Language Edition*, trans. and ed. Burton H. Throckmorton Jr. (Cleveland: The Pilgrim Press, 1992).
4. For an introduction to Etty Hillesum's life and writing, see Etty Hillesum, *An Interrupted Life: The Diaries of Etty Hillesum 1941–43* (New York: Washington Square Press, 1983).
5. For Etty Hillesum's description of how we must make room for both joy and sorrow, see Hillesum, 98–101 and 157–68.
6. Hillesum, 187–88.

22. REFRAINING FROM EXPLAINING

1. George Bernard Shaw, *Saint Joan* (London: Penguin Books, 1957), 106.

23. TELLING THE TRUTH ABOUT OUR LIVES

1. Adrienne Rich, "Women and Honor: Some Notes on Lying (1975)" in *On Lies, Secrets, and Silence* (New York: W. W. Norton and Company, 1979), 193.
2. Ibid.
3. Ibid., 188.
4. Ibid.

24. THE PEARL OF GREAT PRICE

1. For this insight, I am indebted to Rebecca Neal Niese for remarks she made at a Leaven clergywomen's seminar.
2. Heyward, *Touching Our Strength: The Erotic as Power and the Love of God*, 190.
3. Bivens and Richardson, "Naming and Claiming Our Histories," 14.
4. For this distinction between belief *in* Jesus and *believing* him when he speaks about God, I am indebted to Dorothee Sölle and particularly her poem "When He Came" from the collection *Revolutionary Patience* (Maryknoll, N.Y.: Orbis Books, 1977), 16, 17.
5. This last phrase "reconstitute the world" is taken from Adrienne Rich's poem, "Natural Resources," in Adrienne Rich, *The Fact of a Doorframe: Poems Selected and New 1950–1984* (New York: W. W. Norton and Company, 1975), 264.
6. Martin Luther King Jr., *The Words of Martin Luther King Jr.*, selected and with an introduction by Coretta Scott King (New York: Newmarket Press, 1983), 91.

CREDITS

Portions of "Rising like the Phoenix" originally appeared as "Creating Vibrant Churches: Open and Affirming" in *The Chicago Theological Seminary Register*, winter 1994, and "Rising like the Phoenix" in *Open Hands*, spring 1994. Copyright © 1992 by Melanie Morrison.

Sections of "In This *Kairos* Moment" originally appeared in *Created in God's Image: A Human Sexuality Program for Ministry and Mission*, by Eleanor S. Morrison and Melanie Morrison, 69–79. Copyright © 1993 by the United Church Board for Homeland Ministries, Division of the American Missionary Association. Used by permission.

"Remembering Re-Imagining" is adapted from "Here's to You, Mr. Robertson" by Melanie Morrison, in *Re-Membering and Re-Imagining*, edited by Nancy J. Berneking and Pamela Carter Joern. Copyright © 1995 by The Pilgrim Press. Used by permission.

Grateful acknowledgment is given to the editors for permission to reprint material from my essays that originally appeared in these journals:

"A Human Being Fully Alive" is adapted from "Resurrection

Stories: Standing Up and Giving Glory," originally published in *The Other Side*, October 1987.

"A Crisis of Pronouns" is adapted from an article of the same name, originally published in *The Other Side*, March–April 1990. The section on the convergence of events in the Netherlands is drawn from "A Love That Won't Let Go," originally published in *Sojourners*, July 1991.

"Telling the Truth about Our Lives" was originally published in *The Witness*, September 1991.

"The Cross and the Triangle" was originally published in *Leaven Notes*, October 1992.

"Standing on Holy Ground" was originally published in *Leaven Notes*, February 1993.

"Letter to Audre" is adapted from "Remembering Audre Lorde," originally published in *Leaven Notes,* November 1993.

"Singing Hope's Song in a Strange Land" was originally published in *Leaven Notes*, December 1994.

"The Power of Saying God-She" was adapted from an article of the same name originally published in *Lavender Morning*.

BIBLIOGRAPHY

Balka, Christine, and Andy Rose. *Twice Blessed: On Being Lesbian, Gay and Jewish*. Boston: Beacon Press, 1989.

Barndt, Joseph. *Dismantling Racism: The Continuing Challenge to White America*, Minneapolis: Augsburg, 1991.

Bivens, Donna K., and Nancy D. Richardson, "Naming and Claiming Our Histories," *The Brown Papers* (Women's Theological Center in Boston), vol. 1, no. 2 (Nov. 1994).

Boswell, John. *Christianity, Social Tolerance, and Homosexuality: Gay People in Western Europe from the Beginning of the Christian Era to the Fourteenth Century*. Chicago: University of Chicago Press, 1980.

Brock, Rita Nakashima. *Journeys by Heart: A Christology of Erotic Power*. New York: Crossroad, 1988.

Butler, Becky, ed. *Ceremonies of the Heart: Celebrating Lesbian Unions*. Seattle: Seal Press, 1990.

Cannon, Katie G., Beverly W. Harrison, Carter Heyward, Ada Maria Isasi-Diaz, Bess B. Johnson, Mary D. Pellauer, and Nancy D. Richardson. *God's Fierce Whimsy: Christian Feminism and Theological Education*. New York: The Pilgrim Press, 1985.

Christians and Homosexuality: Dancing Toward the Light, 1994. A special issue booklet available from *The Other Side*, 300 W. Apsley, Philadelphia, PA 19144.

Douglas, Mary. *Purity and Danger: An Analysis of the Concepts of Pollution and Taboo*. London: Routledge, 1966.

Frye, Marilyn. *The Politics of Reality: Essays in Feminist Theory*. Trumansburg, N.Y.: The Crossing Press, 1983.

———. *Willful Virgin*. Freedom, Calif.: The Crossing Press, 1992.

Gross, Rita M. "Female God Language in a Jewish Context." In *Womanspirit Rising: A Feminist Reader in Religion*, edited by Carol P. Christ and Judith Plaskow. San Francisco: Harper and Row, 1979.

Heyward, Carter. *The Redemption of God: A Theology of Mutual Relation*. Washington, D.C.: University Press of America, 1982.

———. *Our Passion for Justice*. New York: The Pilgrim Press, 1984.

———. *Touching Our Strength: The Erotic as Power and the Love of God*. San Francisco: Harper and Row, 1989.

Hillesum, Etty. *An Interrupted Life: The Diaries of Etty Hillesum 1941–43*. New York: Washington Square Press, 1983.

Hunt, Mary E. *Fierce Tenderness: A Feminist Theology of Friendship*. New York: Crossroad, 1992.

Johnson, Elizabeth A. *She Who Is: The Mystery of God in Feminist Theological Discourse*. New York: Crossroad, 1994.

Kaufman, Gershen. *Shame: The Power of Caring*. Rochester, Vt.: Schenkman Books, 1980.

Kushner, Lawrence. *Honey from the Rock: Visions of Jewish Mystical Renewal*. San Francisco: Harper and Row, 1977.

Lorde, Audre. *Our Dead Behind Us*. New York: W. W. Norton and Company, 1986.

———. *Sister Outsider*. Trumansburg, N.Y.: The Crossing Press, 1984.

———. *Undersong: Chosen Poems Old and New*. Rev. ed. New York: W. W. Norton and Company, 1982.

Meyerding, Jane, ed. *We Are All Part of One Another: A Barbara Deming Reader*. Philadelphia: New Society Publishers, 1984.

Moraga, Cherríe, and Gloria Anzaldúa, *This Bridge Called My Back: Writings by Radical Women of Color*. New York: Kitchen Table: Women of Color Press, 1981.

Morrison, Toni. *Beloved*. New York: Alfred A. Knopf, 1987.

Morton, Nelle. *The Journey Is Home*. Boston: Beacon Press, 1985.

Nelson, James B. *Body Theology*. Louisville: Westminster/John Knox Press, 1989.

———. *Embodiment: An Approach to Sexuality and Christian Theology*. New York: Augsburg, 1978.

Oosterhuis, Huub, Michel van der Plas, Pius Drijvers, Han Renckens, Franz Jozef van Beeck, David Smith, and Forrest Ingram. *Fifty*

Psalms: An Attempt at a New Translation. London: Burns and Oates; New York: Herder and Herder, 1969.

Plaskow, Judith. *Standing Again at Sinai: Judaism from a Feminist Perspective.* San Francisco: Harper and Row, 1990.

Rich, Adrienne. "Compulsory Heterosexuality and Lesbian Experience." In *Blood, Bread, and Poetry.* New York: W. W. Norton and Company, 1986.

————. *The Fact of a Doorframe: Poems Selected and New 1950–1984.* New York: W. W. Norton and Company, 1975.

————. *On Lies, Secrets, and Silence.* New York: W. W. Norton and Company, 1979.

Ruether, Rosemary Radford. *Sexism and God Talk.* Boston: Beacon Press, 1983.

Schüssler Fiorenza, Elisabeth. *In Memory of Her: A Feminist Theological Reconstruction of Christian Origins.* New York: Crossroad, 1989.

Smith, Barbara, ed. *Home Girls: A Black Feminist Anthology.* New York: Kitchen Table: Women of Color Press, 1983.

Spong, John Shelby. *Living in Sin?: A Bishop Rethinks Human Sexuality.* Nashville: Abingdon Press, 1988.

Thistlethwaite, Susan. *Sex, Race, and God: Christian Feminism in Black and White.* New York: Crossroad, 1989.

Sölle, Dorothee. *Revolutionary Patience.* Maryknoll, N.Y.: Orbis Books, 1977.

Walker, Alice. *The Color Purple.* New York: Washington Square Press, 1982.

INDEX

ableism, 89
abortion, 45–46
accidents, 133–38
Acts, 24
Advent, 17–19
AIDS, 117–18
AIDS quilt, 36, 40–41
Anderson, Dora, 75
anointing with oil, 116–19

baptism, 28–32; of Jesus, 28–29;
    parallels with coming-out rit-
    uals, 39; theology of, 28–30
Barndt, Joseph, 54
Beloved (Morrison), 27–28
Bible: mother-daughter relation-
    ships in, 69–70; patriarchy of,
    69–70
Boswell, John, 33–34
Brown, Antoinette, 80
burning bush, 4–5, 73, 136
Bush, George, 56

Calvinism, 128
celibacy, 20, 25

choice, 35, 97–102, 146
Christian Coalition, 17
Christian community, homosexual
    members of, 20–26
Christianity, 143–47
Christian X, 63
Christmas, 18
church movement, 79–85
circumcision, 24
CLOUT (Christian Lesbians
    OUT Together), 93–94
Colonius, Cyril, 29, 80–81
Color Purple, The (Walker), 59
"coming home," 3–6
coming-of-age rituals, 36
coming out, 12–13, 38–39; par-
    allels with baptism, 39
communion, 118–20, 131–32;
    Jesus and, 119–20
confession, 139–41
Cooney, Julian Richard Day,
    27
covenant service, 40, 84–85
crime, 16
cross symbol, 62–65

death, 103–7; rituals of, 36, 40–41
de Burgos, Julia, 54
delight, expression of, 61
Deming, Barbara, 11
destiny, 127–28
Douglas, Mary, 22

Ecclesiastes, 104
Ecumenical Decade: Churches in Solidarity with Women, 92–93
elections of 1994, reactions to, 14–19
entitlement, 16
Esau, 122
evangelism, 83
exile, 15–19, 34–37, 81

faith, 74, 122
Family Protection Act, 10
feminist theology, 68–74, 92
forgiveness, 140
Frye, Marilyn, 20, 35, 143

Garcia, Marienella, 66, 68
gay men. See homosexuality
German death camps, 62, 63
God: images of, 46–47, 68–74; metaphorical language about, 72–73; name of, 4–6, 47–48, 133–35; nature of, 133–38; oneness of, 24; pain of, 4–5; presence of, 121–26; as She, 45–46, 71; walking humbly with, 58–61
God-She, 45–48, 71
Godwrestling, 121–26
Goldman, Emma, 131
Grace Baptist, 79
grief, 99–100, 103–7
Gross, Rita, 46, 71–72
Gulf War, 56, 141
gun control, 17

happiness, 127–32
healing, and transformation, 121–26
health care reform, 16
healthy narcissism, 29
Heritage Foundation, 17
Heschel, Abraham, 122, 124
heterosexual relationships, openness of, 8, 12, 20–21
Heyward, Carter, 11, 37–38, 73, 144
Hillesum, Etty, 129–30
Hitler, Adolf, 62
holiness, Levitical understanding of, 21–23
holocaust, 64
holy ground, 3–6
homophobia, 8, 95–96
homosexuality: celebration of, 41; choice and, 35; coming out, 12–13; fear and, 8–9; hatred of, 117–18; Jesus on, 21–24, 26; marginality of, 35; membership in Christian community, 20–26; membership in church congregations, 79–85; minority status of gay and lesbian people, 34, 38–39; scripture on, 21–24; secrecy, 7–13; talking openly, 11–12
hope, 143–47
human body, as burden to spirituality, 70
Human Rights Commission (El Salvador), 66
humility, 58–61
Hunt, Earl G., 92–93

internalized homophobia, 8
Iraneus, 88
Isaiah: **43:19**, 67; **48:6–7**, 67; **56:7–8**, 84
Israel, 124

Jacob, 121–26
Jeremiah, 53; **6:13–15,** 49
Jesus, 146–47; baptism of, 28–29; communion and, 119–20; on happiness, 129, 130; healing on Sabbath, 88–89; on homosexuality, 21–24, 26; love of, 30–32; meaning of resurrection and, 86–91; raising Lazarus from dead, 97–102; resurrection of, 66–68, 73–74; and symbol of the cross, 62–65
Jethro, 4
Jewish experience, parallels with homosexual experience, 33–34, 62–63
Joan of Arc, 137
justice, and love, 144–45

kairos, 10, 66–74
Kamphuis, Tine, 75
Kaufman, Gershen, 50–51, 52
King, Martin Luther, Jr., 147

language: inclusive, 68, 71–73; power of, 46–48
Lao Tsu, 129
Lazarus, 97–102
leprosy, 22, 23
lesbian women: and the church, 139–41, 142; and Re-Imagining Conference, 93–96; resurrection of, 92–96. *See also* homosexuality
letting go, 103–7, 125–26
Leviticus, 21–23
liberation theology, 81
life partners, rituals for, 39–40
life passages, 33–41
Limbaugh, Rush, 17
Lorde, Audre, 11, 108–11, 143
love: of Jesus, 30–32; justice and, 144–45; power and limits, 97–

102; of the sinner but not the sin, 25
Luke **13:10–17,** 88–89

MacDonald, George, 124–25
male imagery, 46, 68–74
Mark **7:24–30,** 69
marriage rituals, 36, 39–40
Matthew, 87; **23:23,** 23
Mencken, H. L., 128
Metropolitan Community Churches, 80
Micah **6:8,** 58
Militia, The, 17
More Light Churches Network, 80
Morrison, Toni, 27–28
Morton, Nelle, 70
Moses, 4–5, 73, 115, 136
mother-daughter relationships, in Bible, 69–70
mourning, 103–7

naming, 133–34
Native Americans, 54–55
Netherlands, 9–10, 86–87

oil, anointing with, 116–19
original sin, 82

pain, 4–6
parades, 41
paramilitary organizations, 17
patriarchal theology, 37, 46–47, 69–74
patriarchy, 69–70; of Bible, 69–70; defined, 69
Paul, 27, 81–82
Pellauer, Mary, 71
Peter, and baptism of Gentiles, 24, 79–80
Philip, baptism of eunuch, 23, 79
Phoenix Community Church, 37, 79–85

Plaskow, Judith, 121
Pope, Ludrell, 75
poverty, 17, 54
Prayer of Confession, 82
Presbyterian Layman, 96
pronouns, choice of, 10–11, 46–47, 68
Psalms, 115
Psalm 23, 115–17, 138
Psalm 137, 14–15
purity codes, 21–23
Putnam, Carol, 75

racism, 54–56, 145
Randall, Margaret, 108
redemption, 27–30, 144
Re-Imagining Conference, 92–96
Republican party, 17
resurrection, 66–68, 111; choice of, 97–102; church movement and, 80–85; of Jesus, 66–68, 73–74; of lesbian women, 92–96; liberation as, 86–91; meaning of, 86–91; as standing up and praising God, 88
resurrection faith, 86–91
Rich, Adrienne, 11, 15–16, 140, 141, 143
Richardson, Nancy, 55–56
rites of passage, 33–41
Rites of Passage in America: Traditions of the Life Cycle, 35–36
rituals, 33–41
Robertson, Pat, 92–93, 96, 117
Rushin, Kate, 110–11

700 Club, The, 92–93, 96, 117
sexism, 68–74
sexuality: as gift, 71; shame of, 51–52
shame, 49–57, 140; bad shame, 53–56; defenses against, 52–53; defined, 50–51; of feeling fa-

tigue, 51, 56–57; good shame, 53–56; internalization of, 52–53; of sexuality, 51–52
Shaw, George Bernard, 136–37
sin, 73–74, 82, 144
Sister Outsider (Lorde), 108–9, 111
slavery, 27–28, 80
Sojourner: The Women's Forum, 110–11
Sojourners magazine, 10
Sophia, 75–76, 96
Spirit of the Lakes, 79
spirituality, human body as burden to, 70
Star of David, 62–63
Stonewall insurrection, 41
storytelling, 71
suffering, 64–65, 135, 137
symbols, 62–65

talking openly, 11–12
Temple standards of holiness, 22
Terry, Robert, 54
theology of dualisms, 37–38
transformation, and healing, 121–26
triangle symbol, 62–65
truthfulness, 131–41

Unitarian Universalist church, 84
United Church Coalition for Lesbian and Gay Concerns, 8
United Church of Christ, 82–85

Vietnam War, 56

Walker, Alice, 59
wealth, 54
Wisdom **7:27,** 75
women, in ministry, 80
World Council of Churches, 92
Wounded Knee massacre, 55